Parenting

UNDER Pressure

Voices of prisoners and their families

Editor Adrienne Katz

Listening and responding to young people

Registered Charity No 1078319

The work with prison parents has been supported by
The Family Policy Unit, Home Office.

The work with families of prisoners was supported by
The Diana, Princess of Wales Memorial Fund.

THE WORK CONTINUES

This project was co-ordinated and edited by
Adrienne Katz of Young Voice.

Registered Charity no 1078319

www.young-voice.org

in partnership with

NEW BRIDGE

creating links between the
offender and the community

Published by Young Voice 2002

Foreword Rachel Billington

This book reveals a secret world, a world lived parallel to the ordinary world or that which is considered ordinary by most people, but is hardly known about or understood. Its inhabitants are the prisoners themselves and, in much greater numbers, the families of prisoners. In recording the experiences of family members, it gives a voice to those who are usually unheard but are as involved in the sentencing process as those convicted by law.

Reading it is an extraordinary experience, both uniquely informative and deeply moving. Yet at first it feels as if the reader's entered a large hall filled with voices clamouring for attention. Their desperation makes the noise almost deafening. Mothers, fathers, sons, daughters, grandmothers, grandfathers, sisters, brothers, even some children, each, in just a few sentences, testifies to the effect imprisonment of a loved one has had on their lives. Gradually, they become individual voices, each one suffering and trying to deal with a different mix of difficulties.

Encouraged by the skillful ordering of the material by Adrienne Katz, general themes begin to emerge. Then we begin to see that the grandmother is usually a bulwark for the imprisoned mother, that the non-imprisoned partner, coping with work and children and prison visiting, generally feels she/he is serving a sentence as bad if not worse than her gaoled partner, that what help society offers is either inconsistent or unknown, and that the children are priority for all the family and yet inevitably suffer for the failure of their parents.

This is a world vibrant with unhappiness and pain but also shot through with hope and love. The young fathers are looking forward, many with surprising and perhaps unrealistic confidence, to becoming a responsible father when they are released. Some of the young mothers on the outside are proud to be managing, however great the strain, others despair of keeping the show on the road. The mothers in prison, most often addicts, have more or less given up.

Drink, drugs, violent lack of self-control become themes, whether from the point of view of loyal but disillusioned mothers of much convicted men in their twenties or female partners who hardly dare think about the future. Sadly, the prison attitude to visitors is often criticised. There are some visitors centres which win gratitude and point to change, but too often, particularly first-time prison visitors are upset by their treatment and the unhelpfulness of the system, particularly if accompanied by children. One small example: prison visiting hours seldom fit in with school hours. Criticism also extends to the attitude of barristers and the courts who offer little or no advice or information as a husband, sometimes unexpectedly, is led off for a prison sentence.

Information and support are the key elements to changing this secret world for the better. A first step is to open a door so that those living parallel lives cannot manage to overlook it any longer. For that reason, I would hope that this book will reach a much wider readership than those who work in the penal area. I would hope that it will find its way into libraries, schools, offices and the homes of people fortunate enough to know nothing about its existence.

'Joined up care' is the current buzz word. We need to recognise that planning how to care for the prisoner is a pointless activity unless it is linked to care for his/her family. That is the most important form of joining up. This book makes one thing obvious: the importance of the family, in however untraditional a form, to the welfare of the prisoner and to his behaviour when he returns to society. It is in society's own interests to listen to these voices speaking of turmoil and despair and bring them hope.

FAMILY CHANGE - Chapter four

EMOTIONS - Chapter five

Acknowledgments
This book has been made possible by large numbers of people working together across the country. Many made their contribution anonymously and we are no less grateful to them.

Prison parents.
Interviewing prison parents was carried out through a partnership between Young Voice and The New Bridge – our special thanks go to Ann Renton for working with Adrienne Katz to form this partnership. Lesley Dixon unflaggingly carried out a vast number of interviews with prison parents. Michael Hall transcribed them. There were additional interviews by Jackie Lee and David Stockdale, and further help from Robert Clarke in Scotland. Martin Glynn created a unique resource: 'The Journey of Fatherhood' with young prison fathers in Swinfen Hall. Vital encouragement came from Eric McGraw and Tony Shepherd. Thirty four prisons helped in some way, either with the distribution of questionnaires or opportunities to interview prison parents. Over a hundred prison parents sent in written contributions or offered to participate in an individual interview (71 interviews and over thirty written contributions). The creative writers at Kirklevington Grange and the writer in residence are gratefully thanked for their contributions.

Prisoner's Families.
Visitor's centers were supportive in enabling contact with family members, and Kathryn Walker has undertaken these sensitive discussions, often contacting people several times and arranging to meet in privacy. We are grateful to Sarah Kyte for her valuable interview work with families. Tony Walker, although not officially part of the team, has helped in so many ways. 71 people gave interviews.

347 prison parents kindly answered our questionnaires which were processed and analysed by Alexander Dabbous. We are grateful for his thoughtful and precise work on this project.
Thanks to John Katz for proof reading.

Photographers (photographs sourced by Adrienne Katz)
David Bailey: pages 9,81,90,123,145,150.
Edmund Clark: page 91.
David Mansell: pages 19,42,44,45,52,59,61,67,103,128,137,151,152,153.
Louise Lewer: pages 12,15,16,25,36,88,91,105,109,112,135,141.
The Prison Reform Trust: Cover
The New Bridge: page 123.
Greenock Prison: page 94.
Caroline Penn/Panos Pictures: pages 28, 39.

Speakers in interviews: all names have been changed.
Some photographs are posed by models.

ONE

The
impact on those left behind
and
telling the family

> "I wanted him to know that I was having a prison sentence as well. Yes, he wasn't allowed out at night but I was still in prison and I was the one who couldn't face people. I was the one that was 'taken to prison'. He was told what to do, had a routine, I didn't have a routine but I had to face the newspapers, the family, had to tell people like his Nan and it was awful, the most degrading thing I've ever had to go through."

Mother, whose son served 2 year prison sentence.

THE IMPACT ON THOSE LEFT BEHIND AND TELLING THE FAMILY.

Who suffers most – him or me?

"He says that he suffers most of all because the worst thing going is to lose your liberty, but he's got the security of a roof over his head and three meals a day and on top of that he's got a radio and TV in his cell and he can play badminton and table tennis – he's got it easier than me. I've told him to get lost a couple of times on the 'phone, both times he's agreed to end it, then he's called back and said he's sorry, so I've kept going, really, that's because I don't want to let him down – I love him but I've had enough!"
Teresa 24, supporting her partner who is serving 3 years.

"There were lots of arguments in our family at the beginning. I think the pressure was taken off quite a lot once we started getting some more information about what was going on. I think the not knowing is really hard so you are just banging off each other to try and make sense of it all. I definitely think that it is worse for families than it is for prisoners. I remember having to tell my Nan which was heart breaking, she was in tears. I just wished that my brother could have seen that as I think maybe things could have been different." *Kerrie 24, supporting her brother through his prison sentence.*

"When the verdict came that he was guilty I was hysterical - I wasn't prepared for it at all. I didn't know anything about it. I didn't know where they had taken him to, and I was so frightened. I panicked about the business. I felt numb and overwhelmed. This took its toll on my health, I suffer from chronic fatigue syndrome and I was in and out of hospital constantly - I was so ill. I didn't want anyone to know about what had happened to try and protect the kids."
Elise 35 years old.

What do you tell your child?

There is a real dilemma about this issue. People take very different views and clearly the age of your children and the length of the sentence influence the decision. But some decisions, taken for the best at the time, seem to lock parents into situations they find hard to get out of as the child grows older. When and how do you tell them that the truth is different from what you have been telling them all along? What if they hear it from someone else? Does this affect their trust? Does it make it harder for them to adjust to the news? All this and more is weighed up every day by parents anxious to protect their children.

But once the decision is taken, adults fall into habits: Talking in front of children is one such habit when they are very young, but adults seem to

"I'm not a bad Dad just 'cos I'm a criminal and I want my daughter to know that. I'm not saying it's right what I've done – but I've made those decisions and choices in life."

forget the child does not remain small. Adults spoke in front of children about prison issues even after telling us the child did not know where their father was. And of course children look around them on visits. A child silently waiting could be listening and worrying. What a child imagines may be worse than the truth. Or their 'truth' may differ from someone else's 'truth', as this little story shows:

Two little boys were locked in a fight at a visitors centre. One insisted this was a hospital – his Dad was in hospital. The other was convinced this was the army because that's where he believed his Dad to be. Each would have fought to the end. An older child watching might have stepped in at any moment with 'No, this is a prison stupid'.

In some cases, children were worrying alone because they had realized what the truth was, but could not mention it to anyone as no adult ever talked it through with them. A taboo had set in. The children may overhear anxious adults talking about their parent, they may even be bullied by other children because their parent is inside. Few tell their parents or carers it seems, unless the adults open the door first. A number of prison parents told us that their children have nightmares regularly.

It is common for prison parents to say that if their child asks outright they will tell them the truth – but few children ever do. And what do you say to a child who wonders why their parent has abandoned them? You might be able to talk through some of their fears and reassure them that you, or their parent, still loves them. Grandparents often find themselves having to do this.

Whoever is caring for your child should know and respect your wishes on this. But sometimes it is out of your hands. If a mother is in prison her child might face major upheavals. It may mean moving away from everything familiar – house, school friends and even relatives. For a child whose father is inside, the mother may choose what to say. She may be angry or hurt herself. Will she handle this well? Other adults or children may in turn be very hurtful about the absent parent. No wonder many parents decide to tell their child a different story. But as these speakers show below, agreeing together what you're going to do about this can help.

"There were lots of arguments in our family at the beginning. I think the pressure was taken off quite a lot once we started getting some more information about what was going on."

"When your kids are young you can tell them anything: 'Dad's at work, but we'll see him soon'. But, as they get older you've got to tell them the truth. They will think more of you for it and it's better to find out from you than from some stranger."

W. 44, HMP Wolds, sentence 10 years

Truth or lies?

"We talked a lot in prison with the staff and other men about what point do you tell the truth to your kids? This is one of the biggest issues– what to do for the best? I think it's better to tell the truth. I would feel awful lying to her… She knows, but doesn't talk to anyone else about it. The school knows. We changed schools when I came in this time as we felt it would be better for her. The school is better and seems to deal with the issue. These days there is less stigma about being in prison. I'm not a bad Dad just 'cos I'm a criminal and I want my daughter to know that. I'm not saying it's right what I've done – but I've made those decisions and choices in life."
W. 44, HMP Wolds, sentence 10 years served 2 years 6 months.

"I haven't told my girls I'm in prison. They think I'm at work. Because they're younger it's easier. Their school knows, but they don't. Somehow it works for us all. They were much younger when I was sentenced, so I could tell lies."
J. 24, HMP Wolds, sentence 4 years, served 17 months , parole possible in 8 months. Daughters 6 and 4 years old.

"We felt it best my daughter didn't know where I was. She was told I was in hospital. As I hadn't been well and she knew I had been crying a lot. When I came home the crying would stop. When we talked on the 'phone I tried not to cry. Lying to her was awful but it's the only way I could cope with it which sounds selfish but it was not meant that way. I don't know if I'll ever be able to tell her these things."
Mother 43 years old, 45 days in prison 6 weeks on HDC Long Newton, daughter was 8 years old at the time.

"It may sound daft to you but they don't ask where I am. I don't lie – that's just how it is. Does that make sense? I'm not sure if my kids know where I am, but I don't say the word 'prison'. The kids never comment about where I am. They seem excited about the visits as much as I am. We moved schools because that was the right thing to do. Some other parents are in prison, but the kids never talk about it, that I'm aware of. I don't know what I would say if one came out and asked me directly. I suppose I would tell the truth. I've only tried to protect them. I never wanted to hurt them in any way at all. I know I've lost the best years. I've always loved them and will always love and want them. When people say they love someone, do we know what they mean? It's a word we all use a lot, but what does it mean? I want to protect my kids. Does that mean I love them? I don't know. I need to take one step at a time, in telling them about prison and my life. I've asked each of them separately what they want to do when I go home. It's funny and sad listening to what they said, and it makes me realize that material things don't mean as much. The youngest one wants to go for a

Kentucky Fried Chicken, The middle one wants a holiday to be together. The oldest one wants me there on a Saturday and Sunday when he plays football and all the other Dads are there."
G. 37, HMP Wolds sentence ten years, children aged 9, 8 and 6.

"I have been honest with my children it's the only way to be. We were taught as children we should respect our elders. Our Dutch culture is more strict than in this country. Children do whatever they want to do." *J. 43, HMP Wolds.*

"When your kids are young you can tell them anything: 'Dad's at work, but we'll see him soon'. But, as they get older you've got to tell them the truth. They will think more of you for it and it's better to find out from you than from some stranger." *W. 44 HMP Wolds, sentence 10 years.*

"I never took the kids to see him in prison when they were young, he was only ever in short times and I said he was working away, yes, I lied to them, but when they were older I come clean" *Sue 36, has a daughter 17 and a son 14.*

"Somehow it works for us all. They were much younger when I was sentenced so I could tell lies. They think I'm at work. Because I'm a welder I show then all the metal gates that I've made. I've also made covers for the radiators in the visitors centre. So that's not a lie. I trained as a welder before I came into prison, so in here I have a good job in the workshops. I get the chance to make lots of things for my girls. I always try to give them both a little present, like a picture frame or an ornament. Some children experience bullying if people know their Dad is in prison. That's why I don't want them to know but it's not right lying to them. It's easier when they are younger. I used to work away from home when I was out, so they are used to me being away. One day I will tell them the truth, but at the moment It's the only way I can hold it together. I don't want them to think their Dad is a bad person."
J. 24, HMP Wolds, his daughters are 6 and 4 His sentence 4 years, served 17 months.

"We told the children the truth. We thought it best to. If I said I worked here they would think it OK to be in a place like this. They know I've done wrong and need to be punished for what I've done in the past. I know some blokes tell their kids they are at work, but how long can they tell lies? Kids aren't stupid, they can read and see what's going on around them. The school is aware so they can keep an extra watch on them, but we've had no trouble as yet. They get a lot of support. The nursery has even got my daughter to do a tape to send to me telling me all about her day and what she has done, and what she is going to do. It's lovely to hear her voice whenever I want to."
D. 28, HMP Holme House, has served 2 years of a four and a half year sentence.

"It's not right lying to them... one day I'll tell them the truth. But at the moment it's the only way I can hold it together."

J. 24.

"I told the kids that John's mam had a heart attack and that he was staying with her down south. I had to hide the letters from them because they had HMP Durham stamped on the envelope and they are not stupid, they can read."

Elaine 28, husband John sentenced to 6 months, she has three children aged 11, 4 and 2 years.

What do mothers outside say?

"I didn't really tell the kids about where their Dad was. My youngest, the three year old has learning difficulties anyway and I don't think he would have understood, I think the oldest one clicked on because of what he picked up from other people talking but I didn't want to tell him that his Dad was in prison because then I would have had to start explaining why he was in prison and what he'd done and everything."
Laura 23, visiting her husband doing a three month prison sentence, she has two sons aged 5 and 3 years.

''No way am I telling the kids where their Dad is, they think he's at work, they haven't worked out he's not at work and I aint telling them he's not at work. If they realise he's not at work I'll have to cross that bridge when I come to it but hopefully it wont be for a long time."
Sonya's husband is one year into an eighteen year sentence, they have two children, a son 8 and daughter 4.

When they're older you can't hide it.

"The kids knew what was going on, we sat them down, both of us before Tommy went to court and told them, we explained things."
Lucy 34, visiting her partner Tommy serving a 5 month sentence, she has five children aged 16, 15, 13, 11 and 7 years.

"We have always been very up front with the girls, answered all of their questions honestly and we would never have done anything but tell them the truth. They knew what was going on, I told them that Daddy had a poorly head, it made him try to do bad things and that he was in prison to be punished for that but also that he was in the hospital part of the prison because of his head being mixed up. We had never lied to them about anything and we wanted them to carry on knowing right from wrong."
Jane 38, is the mother of Anne 8 and Mae 6, her husband was remanded in custody.

Complex stories

"It was hard not telling the kids but he didn't want them to know, he didn't want them to see him in there and I wouldn't have wanted to take them, I was past myself having to visit and didn't want to put them through that. I told the kids that John's mam had a heart attack and that he was staying with her down south. I had to hide the letters from them because they had HMP Durham stamped on the envelope and they are not stupid, they can read. I hated lying to them, John would 'phone sometimes when they were at school and I would tell them about the call, they would say – can he not 'phone back later? No one knew, so no one

could have told them. If it had been the kind of thing to make the papers we would have both discussed it with them before John went to court, we would never have put them in the position of finding out from someone else. If it had been for longer we would have told them as well."
Elaine 28, husband John sentenced to 6 months, she has three children aged 11, 4 and 2 years.

Grandmothers

"The kids didn't go to see him ever, I don't know what they would have decided if he had been away for longer but as it was a short time they told the boys that Dad was working away. John missed his children so much that I don't think he'll ever re-offend. They just think it's great that he's back home from work. The school or no one knew, we didn't say anything." *Sandra (grandmother) had three sons in prison at the same time, she is still visiting Robbie 25.*

"We told the kids the truth from the start but when Bob and me come back from court the day she was sentenced I couldn't face telling them, Bob told them, then I did what I could with them but they didn't make a lot of noise about it, they took it in a quiet kind of way'."
Geraldine is a grandmother taking care of her daughter's two children while their mother serves a ten year sentence.

Who tells and how much?

"My ex-partner hasn't told her yet or I don't know if she will. I would rather be the one to tell her. I don't believe in telling lies to a child, but we just don't mention it on visits. If she asks me outright I would give her the truth but until then we will wait. I don't know if that's the right thing to do, but it's what's best for now." *M.25, HMP Loudham Grange, sentence 8 years served four. Daughter aged 4.*

"I think about what and how much their Mam has told them, but I'll never know."
R.42, sentence 9 years served 3. Loudham Grange two daughters aged 14 and 16.

"My granddaughter came home from school the next day. She had no idea. (We didn't even know my daughter was going to court). She was told Mum was in hospital. That's what she wanted her to know. The probation officer rang to see if I needed anything. What did I need? I didn't know anymore. But our granddaughter was always around so we couldn't talk. I didn't want to go to the shops in case anyone said something or knew something. I didn't go to Church. I didn't feel clean enough to go. But yet I had to do all these things for my granddaughter. She needed to survive in a normal way. That was the hardest part. Keeping it from her. But we did. We didn't want her to know her Mum was in prison. The first time she 'phoned it was awful. I wanted to get hold of her but was also mad. Why didn't she tell me? Why did she do it? There are so many unanswered questions. I kept looking at my granddaughter and crying. It was

the school holidays so we had to keep a ten year old amused. My daughter used to write to her everyday and she used to write to her Mum maybe two or three times a week. That was really difficult 'cos we couldn't let her put the address on the envelope. So I had to get up before her every morning and put the address on the envelope and post it. I kept thinking it was a dream and I was babysitting for a few days. How people cope for any length of time I don't know. If she would have been given a longer sentence I don't know how we would have pretended any longer. I know we didn't have the right to stop our granddaughter going to visit but we felt it would have been wrong for her to see her Mum there. It was all lies. She's a bright child and wanted to know why she couldn't go to hospital to see her Mum, but we kept saying she needed rest. And when she 'phoned we wanted to talk to her but couldn't say things in front of her daughter and she kept saying 'Can't we 'phone Mum? Why do we have to wait for her to 'phone us?' It was all a pretence and lies and that's the difficult bit – I was drained. My husband went to see her with her partner every week. He looked so pathetic when he got home. They both did. They didn't tell her daughter they had seen her as she would have wanted to go – so again it was more lies."
Sally, her daughter was given a six month sentence and she and her husband cared for their granddaughter.

"We thought people in prison were given probation officers, she doesn't have a probation officer, we're told that she won't have one 'til it's nearly time for her to get out, but we don't know when that will be. We can't give the kids any idea when their mother will get out because they tell us that she won't be eligible for parole until she starts doing courses, but how can she do courses when they keep moving her around? She can't settle anywhere long enough to do any courses so we can't tell the kids what year she might get out. They won't give us any straight answers so how can we give straight answers to the kids?"
Geraldine, coping with her 2 grandchildren while her daughter serves a ten year sentence.

"It has been an absolute nightmare for me and my three children. Me and my wife were arrested for conspiracy to commit murder, the children were so devastated. We decided not to tell them everything - they know bits of it but how do you explain something like this to them?"
Stuart 32, his wife received a prison sentence.

How do children take it?

"We had to be careful how we told him, but Lee knows what his Dad's in for, we wanted him to know what he'd done wrong and why he was in there. For that first year Lee was having nightmares and wouldn't sleep or eat and things, but he's OK now. He gets excited about going, at first he used to go all quiet in the car when we were leaving but now he's happy with it. It's not a place for kids but there's another two years left on top of the four that he's done and Lee could have gone bad through not having a Dad."

Alice, a grandmother who takes Lee to see his father.

"I didn't tell the kids at first, I thought that I was doing that to protect them but I didn't want to lie to them and thought that I should sit them down and tell them – I felt I should do that. This was two weeks after he went away, my daughter said 'I wish you'd told me straight away, I feel better now not thinking that Dad's working away, I don't care as long as I can go to see him, loads of the kids at my school have Dads in prison, it doesn't matter as long as I know where he is and I can see him'. I think that it was during those first two weeks I had to get my head round things, I had to accept it first before I could tell the kids."

Jackie 37, supports husband Paul, sentenced to three and a half years, they have three children aged 9 and 5 years, the baby is 7 months.

"Mae told everyone –'Daddy's in prison, when the kids told the class on Mondays what they had done over the weekend, Mae would tell them that she'd been to prison to see Daddy, the eight year old was more conscious, more guarded. Their friends were very good, asking how their Dad was, they didn't lose friends, didn't get stick because of it." *Jane 38, her husband was remanded in custody – they have two children, Anne 8 and Mae, 6.*

"My eldest daughter didn't go on the day he got sentenced. To be honest, with all the reports, for some reason we really didn't believe he would get a custodial sentence. She was devastated. She couldn't get the time off work, we did reassure her, she was going to go anyway but we reassured her that he would be back home later. So there was my youngest daughter, his sister and me. When they sentenced him, I mean I have never seen my youngest daughter so upset." *Trudi 40.*

"My son is very quiet, he gets embarrassed about his Dad, you have to draw things out of him, and he doesn't enter into any conversation about him. 'When he started secondary school he sat on the field with his new school friends and said my Dad's on drugs, I asked why he'd told them that? He said well, if they're ever walking down the road with me and see him they'll know anyway so I just wanted it out in the open."

Sue 36, her ex partner and father of her two children is now released from prison.

"They knew I was in prison. My youngest used to have nightmares after she came to visit me. The prison was called Castle and she thought I was locked up in the dungeon. Her behaviour became odd and she is seeing a psychologist at the school."

R.42, HMP Loudham Grange serving 9 years, his daughter is 14 now but was much younger when he was in before.

> **"My son is very quiet, he gets embarrassed about his Dad, you have to draw things out of him, and he doesn't enter into any conversation about him."**
>
> *Sue 36, her ex partner and father of her two children is now released from prison.*

What the children say:

"School's been all right for me, I have lots of good friends. I didn't have to tell them about my Dad 'cos they found out from what was printed in the paper. They didn't say much about it….they didn't dare 'cos I wouldn't stand for it! They know that they can't bully me else they'd get a smack. The worst bit was going to see him at the Dana as they search you quite a lot, I didn't really like that. The best bit has been when my Dad gets town visits 'cos you get a longer time with him and you can go shopping and stuff. I've got on all right with my Dad as he kept telling me that he was all right, we talked quite a lot on the 'phone. I've never been angry with him - I was really just pleased to have him home."
Nicky 14, his Dad is serving a prison sentence.

"I'm wearing my new earrings to go and see Mum and a bit of lipstick because I don't want her to think I'm letting myself down, you know, that I'm keeping smart. She writes letters sometimes but she sends cards mostly, I like her cards and I don't think she likes writing lots of letters".
Sarah 11, her Mum is serving a ten year sentence.

"When I come here I like to play on the slide, I wish they would do baked potatoes at weekends and I would like it if you'd let my Mum come home please."
Adam 7, visiting his Mum, he lives with Grandma while his mother is serving a ten year prison sentence.

"I missed him loads…. It was my birthday 2 days after he went away which was horrible. Me and my sister we bought a puppy at Christmas so that when we had town visits we could take him for a walk with Dad like we used to before he went away."
Claire 15, keeping contact with her Dad in prison.

My Dad's in Prison
A series of information and support leaflets for families of prisoners

My Dad's in Prison—What about Me?
A poster-style sheet for older children and young people to express their feelings about their father's imprisonment.

My Special Book:
I'm going to visit my Dad in Prison
A booklet for younger children to fill in with drawings or words when preparing to visit their father. It encourages the child to think about the journey, the visit and what they might like to say to their father.

What Shall I Tell the Children?
for adults about talking to children about their father
Visiting Prison with Your Children
preparing a child to visit

Still a father figure...

"I think you should be honest with the kids. If they don't find out from us there will be people who want to tell them and make it worse than it is. They know their Dad loves them. They don't write every week but they write now and again to let him know what's going on. One of the girls has started her periods and she actually wrote him a letter to tell him. I didn't know what to think but she thought I would be embarrassed to tell him and she thought it better in a letter."
Melanie

"It is worse being inside being a parent than on the out. If anything was to happen to any of them while I was in here I would feel terrible - a worse Dad than I am. When I was at home something happened to one of my girls but I was there for her. But if I had been in here it would have been worse. I call my kids. The ones from my second marriage, the ones from my first marriage are older and able to look after themselves, but I still worry about them and the grandkids".
E. 46, HMP Kirklevington Grange. He has 9 children ranging from 9 years old to 24.

"I came into prison soon after my son was born. Now I get out every Sunday and take my lad into town. I saw his first steps in Durham nick and watched him grow and develop while I've been banged up, and that can't be right. That's why on town visits I make a real fuss of him. I 'phone him every day. If he's not at our house he'll be at his gran's either my Mam or our lass's mother. He's got asthma and I worry myself sick about it. Every day I ask him if he's taken his inhaler – that's the first thing I say to him! When meningitis was rife I couldn't stand the worry in case he got it. I told his Mam to make sure he got all his injections. It's awful being separated and things like this happen. I would always keep 'phoning so he knows my voice and who I am. It's only right a kid should know who his Dad is. I don't want to be a stranger like a lot of the blokes in here. A lot of blokes worry about what their lass is up to – they forget about the kids. He is my life."
H. 32, HMP Kirklevington Grange sentence 6 years, he has served three. His son is three and a half years old.

Will my child still want to know me?

"You should always tell the truth to them no matter what age. It's best. My youngest son is a good lad. Not a cruel type. I love to see him and talk to him. He knows why I'm here, but he doesn't think I'm a bad Dad. I feel I am close to my son, but it's such a long time to be away from him. I don't know how things will turn out. I pray that he still wants to know me."
D. 37, HMP Wolds on a 12 year sentence. His 5 children are aged 10 –20, one in UK, others in Jamaica.

"It's only right a kid should know who his Dad is. I don't want to be a stranger like a lot of the blokes in here. A lot of blokes worry about what their lass is up to – they forget about the kids. He is my life."

H. 32, HMP Kirklevington sentence 6 years, he has served three. His son is three and a half years old.

"I've known some men who are frightened to get in touch with their kids, but that's not right. There are people in the jail to help."

E. HMP Kirklevington Grange aged 46. sentence 4 years, 14 months served. E has nine children aged between 9 and 24.

"The probation social worker staff see my kids. They have assessments done on them. They are asked about their Dad. All they say is it was brilliant when he was at home and it will be brilliant when he comes home. The lads are good really, and they do help me talk about things. We wonder how things went wrong. But we can't live in the past. We have to move on for everyone's sake."
C. two teenage sons aged 17 and 13 years, their father is serving a sentence.

"My son is so loyal to me. He used to visit all the time, now I get home visits weekly. I see him each Sunday and we spend time together. He hates it when I see people I know from the past that still do drugs, but I think he's starting to trust me. That's the main thing. I think kids have to know they can trust their parents. He has never been able to, but now we are starting to have that kind of relationship, but it takes time to prove he can trust me. I know my drug problem is solved. The prisons have helped, but I know it's not going to be easy out there. I am trying to be realistic. I know my son and my wife don't get on. I don't know what to do, but I know I have to put my son's needs before my own otherwise what message am I giving him?"
C. HMP Kirklevington Grange age 35 with son of 16.

"I've known some men who are frightened to get in touch with their kids, but that's not right. There are people in the jail to help. Probation and the Chaplaincy are great. If you've got no money at Christmas time the chaplain will arrange for a present to be sent for your kids and it's wrapped properly and not slapping of prison property."
E.. HMP Kirklevington Grange, aged 46, sentence 4 years, 14 months served. E has nine children aged between 9 and 24.

"As the time came nearer for me to go home I couldn't believe I would be seeing her – what it would be like. I missed her smell, brushing her hair. I thought of all the times I had shouted at her and let her down. The pain really made me feel physically sick. I was a failure – how could she ever respect me? My release date was set four days before her birthday which was better than winning the lottery. I was desperate to see her – to touch her – kiss her goodnight and be able to talk to her. I think back now and wonder if I needed her more than she needed me?"
Mother 43, of ten year old daughter, Low Newton.

"I want to get on better with my daughter but I don't know how to or if she wants to."
S. 46, mother of four and two grandchildren serving four years in Low Newton.

Telling the school

"I did go to the school and spoke to the headmaster but I don't think that they were that bothered. The kids haven't really mentioned it to many people only to their closest friends, the oldest keeps asking when he's coming home which is difficult to understand, 8 years seems like an eternity to me let alone what it must seem like to a child." *Angie 27.*

"I wont tell them, I haven't told the school, I don't want them to know, I don't want the school to know. If the kids knew they'd tell everybody and I don't want anybody to know, It's my own business."
Sonya's children are 8 and 4 years old.

"The school's done nothing to support us and they gave a talk on drugs and the other kids had a go at our two because they all know what Paula's in for because it was in the papers and on the local news."
Geraldine, grandmother of Adam and Sarah.

"I went to the school to see the headmistress; I knew that she would be aware anyway because it had been made very public. She was very good, very accommodating, it's not exactly an everyday occurrence in that school for someone's Daddy to go to prison, where we live it is very unusual. The teachers took time out every day to offer the girls a moment if they wanted to talk about anything, I kept the school up to date." *Jane 38, mother of Anne 8 and Mae 6.*

"I didn't tell the school – didn't want to broadcast it, no one has teased or picked on Gemma, I made sure she understood that if she was having problems at school through it she should tell me, kids can be nasty can't they? But she's had no problems. I don't feel like I have needed support from the school but I would have gone and talked with them if I did need support but it's a need to know basis and her work hasn't suffered."
Jackie 37, mother of 9 year old Gemma and two other children aged 5 years and 7 months.

"The children surprised me as they did really well in school, they felt loved and they never complained. It was very hard for them, it was probably harder for them as they had to go to school everyday and face everyone when I didn't. I just cocooned myself in the house and tried to keep out the outside world. The deputy head master was a magistrate, I spoke to the school and explained the situation but to be honest they didn't really have much of an idea about what to do or how they could make things easier for the children. I think that the schools need educating a lot more about this. At the moment they are not clued up."
Elise 35,

"The school's done nothing to support us and they gave a talk on drugs and the other kids had a go at our two."

Geraldine, grandmother of Adam and Sarah.

> "**The nursery has even got my daughter to do a tape to send to me telling me all about her day and what she has done, and what she is going to do. It's lovely to hear her voice whenever I want to.**"
>
> *D. 28, HMP Holme House, has served 2 years of a four and a half year sentence.*

"The preschool teacher of my youngest daughter was very helpful - she wrote a letter to the judge saying how upset my daughter was by the whole thing. The other teachers had words with the bullies at school, which did help a bit. They have actually managed quite well through school. They only see their Mum at weekends so they don't miss anything. At one point they missed 2 afternoons a month when she was put into a different prison."
Stuart 32, father of three children, his wife is serving a prison sentence.

"My daughter's school were really good, I went in to see the headmaster and he really understood. All the school reports that came back were brilliant; they all said how proud of her they were. The headmaster said to us that some people use things like this as an excuse to bunk off school, not do the work, but my daughter got stuck in. That was all she did, she did brilliantly in school."
Trudi 40, son sentenced to 22 months.

"The kids from school read about my Dad in the newspaper - then they kept asking me all about it which I didn't like - I fell out with most of my friends as they were horrible to me. I wasn't really interested in work when my Dad was away, I've had lots of bad school reports, I didn't like going. The teachers weren't very understanding about it they didn't really care or do anything about everyone picking on me. I ended up staying off school quite a lot 'cos I didn't want to go. My younger sister is much louder and more confident than me, she did fall out with a few friends but she was a lot tougher and didn't really care. It bothered me more."
Claire 15, her Dad was in prison.

"The kids have suffered so much, most days they cry for their Mum. I went to the school and spoke to the headmaster, but he wasn't really that interested. The other kids picked on them saying 'Your Mum's a murderer', as they had read about it in the papers. There was lots of village gossip as well."
Stuart 32, wife received a prison sentence.

"Their teachers know. It's the oldest one I worry about most. We live in a naff estate and I know he's probably doing things he shouldn't be. He does go to school so I should be grateful. We do take an interest in school but who knows what will happen? They seem to accept it. They do ask when will Dad be home? Mainly the younger ones. They don't realise time do they? He's missed most birthdays this year and Christmas, but he should be home for the next one if all goes well. I feel I've let the kids down but I haven't broken the law really, but I suppose I knew what he was up to. We want to change but around here it is hard. We are lucky we are still all together and we are healthy. But I don't want this life forever. I don't want my kids to go inside when I hear the tales he tells of some cons and staff." *JT. Visits husband in HMP Durham. They've been married eighteen years and have four children. He has been inside before.*

I don't know anyone who has been in prison before.

"I don't know anyone who has been in prison before. This has been the first experience I have had with it. I can't begin to tell you how it feels. Part of me has died and it will never come back. I know that might sound silly specially as my daughter is at home now, but something went from me when this happened and will never be the same. I still love her, probably more. But it is so devastating it feels like a death inside.

I didn't know my daughter was going to prison. I didn't even know she was in court. She told me something was wrong but not all the details. I found out from her friend that she was in trouble. But she kept saying everything would be OK nothing would happen.

There were so many bad times before she went to prison and now looking back I can understand why she must have been terrified but could not talk to anyone. Fear of not knowing what would happen to her or her daughter? I had no idea - my husband and I had no idea. Were we to blame? Should we have known? I don't know. She never told anyone she was in court. She made arrangements for our grand daughter to stay with a friend from school that night as it was at the end of term. I knew nothing till her partner came to the door. I thought they were dead by the look on his face. Well we then found out. She had been sentenced to 6 months in prison. All we could think of was our grand daughter. What could we tell her? How would we cope? What would we have to do? Would our grand daughter's Dad come and take her from us? Would social workers be involved? We all just felt sick. We rang the prison. They were helpful. We had no idea what to do. I couldn't talk. I was terrified. I have never felt like that in my life and I have had quite a few experiences, but this was indescribable. I didn't want to go and see her in prison. I felt it would kill me. My husband went and it broke his heart - when he got home that hurt. He is a strong man but this broke him. I am not the type to ask for professional help but I felt desperate at the time." *Sally, daughter in prison cared for her granddaughter.*

"We've been together 17 years, married 15 and we have two sons 17, and 13 years old. This is the first time anyone in our family has gone to prison – but I know of other people round us who've been sent down. You know you've just got to get on with it. It's crap. I exist. I don't have a life. You've got to be strong and plod along for everybody else. I suppose you forget about yourself. I don't think my life will ever be normal again. It's the last thing on your mind at night and the first thing when I wake up and I don't stop thinking about it in between. I take anti-depressants. I suppose they must help. I don't know if they do or not. Most of the women you talk to in the visitors centre are on tablets or drink too

"I don't want this life forever. I don't want my kids to go inside when I hear the tales he tells of some cons and staff."

JT. Visits her husband in HMP Durham. They've been married eighteen years and have four children. He has been inside before.

"You know you've just got to get on with it. It's crap. I exist. I don't have a life. You've got to be strong and plod along for everybody else. I suppose you forget about yourself. I don't think my life will ever be normal again."

C, mother of two sons 17 and 13. her husband is in Acklington with a 7 year sentence.

much. What kind of a life is this? I don't like the situation at all. We have all been affected by what my husband has done. Because of what he did he got a 7 year sentence. He admitted his guilt. He should get parole and be out in 2004. It's about 110 visits. Yes it was wrong and awful what he did and we are all paying the price for it. Nobody explains what to do on a visit and you are in a state of shock anyway. Now we are used to the routine. I don't know how anyone could have helped me. I can't even think that I would ever be in this situation. How sad am I? I've questioned myself so much. I've blamed myself. I don't know what to think. We've been together so long, I had no idea – we are never apart except when he is at work. I worry about it but I am facing it and I think that is what others in my situation should do."

C, mother of two sons 17 and 13. her husband is in Acklington with a 7 year sentence.

"We have always been law abiding and have both worked since we were 16. Michael was involved in an incident, it happened at work and he is suffering from posttraumatic stress disorder. He was put under arrest and sent to prison. I was absolutely devastated, that's the only way that I can describe it. A friend of ours went to see him first, he found everything out and showed me the ropes, he even booked my first visit for me. It was well over a week before I saw him, I went up there by myself and emotions were running extremely high, I'd never been to a prison before, I had never known anyone who'd been to prison before, I hadn't even been to a police station, we'd never even had a parking ticket."

Jane is 38, her husband was remanded for five months, They have two children.

"I didn't know anything about the arrest at first. At that time I only ever saw him when he wanted money. I was shocked as it involved other relatives living in the same village. I was devastated when I found out. He didn't want us to come to the hearings. The police rang the house and told my partner the crimes. We just couldn't believe he'd done them."

Jill 47.

Contact

"Although I do not have as many visits now as I did at my previous prison, due to the distance involved, the time I do spend with my daughter is really quality time. I forget my cares and come back from the visit happy, smiling and feeling somehow re-vitalised."

CHAPTER TWO CONTACT

Can you be an effective father in prison?

"Obviously there are enormous difficulties which must be overcome if you are to even attempt to be an effective father whilst in prison. The main problem is clearly the fact that you just aren't there! You aren't there for day-to-day problems and emergencies that will face your family at home. You will not be there when your child needs help with her education and homework. Equally important – you are not there to share the little triumphs like appearing in the school play or winning a race at Sports Day. You will also not be there for Christmas and birthday celebrations, holidays, walks in the park, trips to the zoo and all those many, many wonderful times that make being a Father to your child such a wonderful experience. Of course all these problems are, often the same, or similar to those faced by any absent parent. The prison father/child relationship must, however also face a whole host of other problems which are specific to only this type of relationship.

Some fathers in prison may have other problems and issues related to the actual sentence they are serving and the prison environment in which they are living. By letting this affect his relationship with their children they will possibly appear unfeeling or false, both of which are things children pick up on very quickly. He will often build psychological 'walls' within the prison, and may have difficulty in lowering these 'walls' when dealing with his family. The prison father may have limited communication with his children anyway, maybe difficulty writing letters and not being able to 'phone as often as he would like. It is also sometimes the case that prison machismo, or even embarrassment might hinder his interaction with his children when he is on a visit, thereby spoiling what should be a happy time for everyone.

For someone doing a short sentence – none of these problems is so great. They have the option of dropping out of their child's life for a relatively short period of time and simply taking up where they left off upon their release. For somebody doing a long time however, this choice is simply not available. To be an effective father in this situation requires love, thought, effort, consideration, determination and above all these, the desire to be an effective father, the need to be a major part of your child's life. In short to be an effective father while you are in prison you must be prepared to work at it!

In my opinion, the key to being an effective 'prison tather', in all aspects of your relationship with your child, is communication. Not just the quantity of communication, how many visits or how many 'phone calls you have, but the quality – how you interact with your child when you are in contact. You must be prepared to listen to what they say. No matter how trivial it may seem to you, it is obviously important to them or they wouldn't be telling you, and consequently important to you too. You've got to interact and communicate freely on your visits. Forget everything else as it seems much better to try to put your own problems aside; prison life is nothing to do with your family, just take what joy you can in your children and enjoy being with them for the short time you've got. I feel I am a fairly effective father to my daughter – as close a relationship as many fathers who are actually outside. Although I do not have as many visits now as I did at my previous prison, due to the distance involved, the time I do spend with my daughter is really quality time. I forget my cares and come back from the visit happy, smiling and feeling somehow re-vitalised.

I try to 'phone home every night and take an interest in her education - her various projects and constantly telling her how proud I am of her achievements, be they something minor or important. If she is taking exams I will try to 'phone her before with encouragement, I am very careful not to criticize her in any way, reassuring her that I am happy with her progress as long as she does her best. I think because of this and the effort my wife puts in at home of course, my daughter seems to enjoy making us proud. On rare occasions when I 'phone she is deeply involved in a game with her friends. Even then she will come to the 'phone to tell me she loves me, and promising to speak to me the next day. I don't find this upsetting in any way. I feel it shows the strength of our relationship that she feels able to do this and we finish every conversation no matter how short or how long by telling each other 'I love you' and both go away feeling happy and content.

I also write to her every week. Recently she has become interested in bird watching so when I can, I compose a letter on the computer decorating it with different pictures of birds and telling her of my own bird watching adventures as a child. She comes on the 'phone all excited and identifies all the birds.

I am not trying to hold myself up as a shining light of fatherhood (if I was, I would be out there with her) and I know my relationship with my daughter is not perfect! The thing is, I genuinely want to be as effective a father as it is possible for me to be in my present situation. She is reassured that I have not abandoned her. There is absolutely no doubt in her mind that I love her. She is happy and well balanced - I can only assume I am doing something right. The thing to remember is that it is not a one-way thing, the harder you are prepared to work, the more you put in, the more you will get out of the relationship. I have found that by doing the best job I can, even while in prison, not only can I be a reasonably effective father, but I derive so much enjoyment and sense of well-being from my relationship with my daughter, it helps me get through my sentence." *This written contribution came from W. in HMP Wolds, Everthorpe. He has a daughter of 8 years old and he and his wife work hard at their daughter's security. He is 44 and serving 10 years. He has served 2 years 6 months.*

"I must admit I still get a lump in my throat when I say 'bye, and she is waving to me. She's got used to me now - but that has been hard work by all of us. You have to 'phone every day. She needs to know I'm her Dad."

"But it's my baby boy I'm worried about. His mother used to visit me with him but now my mate brings him in each month. I haven't seen him for 2 months now. I've found out she's getting married to someone else."

N. 40, HMP Kirklevington, sentence 3 years 6 months due out on HDC, his baby son is fourteen months old.

"I got out of prison the day after she was born. It's been difficult for my girlfriend but she has stood by me and copes really well. It was strange seeing this little thing for the first time; it was unreal, knowing it was mine. A lot of my mates have kids, but it was funny thinking I had one. I have been in and out of prison."
T. 20, Kirklevington Grange.

"I knew it would be difficult for visiting but my girlfriend came every week with the baby and I've watched her grow up through prison life. I've always 'phoned every day to talk to both of them. The visits were much better here - more friendly for children considering it's still a prison; they try hard. I send my daughter a 'miss you' card every week and I've had home visits for a while so I get to see her life too. I must admit I still get a lump in my throat when I say bye, and she is waving to me. She's got used to me now - but that has been hard work by all of us. You have to phone every day. She needs to know I'm her Dad."
D.20, HMP YOI Brinsford, his daughter is 3.

"I was only twenty years old when she was born. I'm still with her mother and they are my life. We were happy when we had our baby girl. I get on really well with her - I spent a lot of time with her - and still do when I see her now. I feel parents need to build bridges with their children, even on the out it's not easy but it's worse in here as they have their life and you have to get on and accept your lot while you are at Her Majesty's pleasure. I've told my daughter where I am. I don't believe in telling lies. As a parent you should be as honest as you can be. I feel choked when I think about the time I've missed out in her life. I can't resist cuddling her when I see her. It's good to write to your own child even if they can't read. You can draw pictures or colour in things. When I only had the one hour visit that was hard – watching her wave, but there's nothing you can do except look forward to the next visit."
P. 24, HMP Kirklevington Grange, daughter 4 years.

"she was 28 days old when I first saw her. Then I didn't see her again until she was 1 year old." *M.25, HMP Loudham Grange sentenced 8 years, served 4.*

Are you in contact with the mother?

YES
73% of men aged 22 or less
83% of men aged 23 and above

NO
26% of men aged 22 or less.
15% of men aged 23 and above

FATHERS: do you keep contact with your child?

Fathers aged 22 or less.
YES 64% receive visits, 46% write to their child, 49% 'phone their child, 38% keep contact through the mother.

Fathers aged 23 and above:
YES 69% receive visits, 65% write to their child, 57% 'phone and 25% keep contact through the mother.

MOTHERS:
52% were in contact with the children's father
68% felt their children were being well looked after,
30% had no say in these arrangements.
49% of their children had no say either.
46% of mothers were in contact with their children,
80% wrote letters,
73% 'phoned .
But 7% of children did not want to visit.

Taken from the Young Voice survey 2001

No contact with your child's mother
"I know my older kids (15 and 16) are fine with their mother; she's a good mother to them. I will see them more often and I know it will be fine. I'm not saying perfect but I think we can pick up the pieces They know me but I don't want them to see me in here. But it's my baby boy I'm worried about. His mother used to visit me with him but now my mate brings him in each month. I haven't seen him for 2 months now. I've found out she's getting married to someone else. I think she's mad but I worry about the baby. I think I'll get custody of him.

"I wish, like others, I'd never got into this mess - but I did, and I've made a mess of everything, but my kids know I love them. "

"The girls don't see their real Dad. I had nobody to help me. I lived alone. Each weekend my Dad would have them for a while. I want to get them back but nobody will trust me. I can't talk to anyone in here. I've had to tell lies about why I'm here."

Mother denied access to her children.

My mate says the baby goes to anyone; he hardly talks much. That bothers me; it's all been out of my control since I've been in the nick. You only get snippets of info from mates, but I'm out soon. I'm going back to live with my mother, which will be funny as I left home at 17. But I need a stable address for tagging and I want my baby back. I need to. My girlfriend sold all the furniture in the house. I think she needs the money to feed her new boyfriend's drug habit. I'm worried if my baby has watched what's going on, he's still young but he shouldn't be in that atmosphere. My family see my ex-girlfriend out in the town but she never has the baby with her. I don't know who has him. I can't tell the social services in case they take the baby off her, and then what chance have I got to get him back? I have to depend on others to see him; it's usually my mate that brings him in. He's too young to write to; I can't even phone him as she's had the phone cut off. I'm boiling inside but what can I do until I get out? I think it would be easier to keep contact with your children when you're in jail if you have a good relationship with the mother. You need to be adult and not on drugs. I love it when I do see him but I don't think he is developing like he should. She doesn't care and I have no say yet. I wish things had been different but I'll have to work to get it right again. He'll have a canny life if I get my way and he's young enough to forget the life he has had so far." *N. 40, HMP Kirklevington Grange, sentence 3 years 6 months due out on HDC, his baby son is fourteen months old.*

"I've been married twice, divorced from my first wife, remarried and split up from my second wife four years ago. I have 9 kids: eight daughters and one boy. My kids from my second wife don't see me as much as she's with another bloke and he tells them I'm no good, even though he was in the same prison as me before - we were kept separate just in case anything happened. I wish, like others, I'd never got into this mess - but I did, and I've made a mess of everything, but my kids know I love them. My first wife doesn't bother as the kids are older, but my second wife is trying to turn them against me, so it's even harder to keep the relationship going. But I'll go and see them as soon as I can. I know it isn't easy but we can't give up. I get lots of letters from the girls but I last saw my son ten months ago. My eldest daughter comes to see me every two weeks. I write to them or 'phone, but it's not the same trying to put your feelings into words. It's hard writing letters but it's all you can do."
E. HMP Kirklevington aged 46. Serving four years, served fourteen months. His 9 children range from 9 years old to 24 and he has three grandkids.

"It's difficult like, 'cos her Mum don't bring her to see me. 'Cos I've only seen her like about twice since I've been here. She's playing games with it and wants solicitors and that. But when she does come up I feel good and I'm just holding her and that." *Young offender, Swinfen Hall.*

When a mother is denied access to her children

"I made the biggest mistake ever leaving my girls with someone I thought I knew. I was found guilty of not protecting them, guilty of not seeking medical advice when I should have. My Dad took the girls to hospital. I had an OK childhood, it wasn't perfect. My Mam and Dad divorced. I'm closer to my Dad. When I get out I'll see more of him, but he's ill and I'm not sure if he'll be alive. He doesn't visit me, it's too far. I'll never be allowed to see my children again, they were fostered after this happened. They are together. I thought they had fallen down while trying to walk but they had lots of bruises so Dad took them to hospital. I really had no say in what was going on. They have now been adopted, but I've refused to sign the papers' cos I want to get them back. I need to clear my name and get him prosecuted. I met the adoptive parents for 15 minutes and I didn't like them but they have my girls. The girls don't see their real Dad. I had nobody to help me. I lived alone. Each weekend my Dad would have them for a while. I want to get them back but nobody will trust me. I can't talk to anyone in here. I've had to tell lies about why I'm here. There are some staff I can talk to but what good can anyone do?

I feel sick when I think about it all. The girls were good for me 'cos when I was pregnant I gave up drugs and alcohol and cigs, but I went back on the cigs. It was an awful violent relationship. I know when I get out I will go back onto the drugs and drink as it will help to blot things out.

It has destroyed my trust in everyone. You have to be careful who you trust especially with your children and I don't know the people who have my girls. I've made such a big mistake. I feel like ending it all sometimes. I worry about them so much but I can't do anything. I'm not allowed to contact them. I can only write once a year and I haven't done that yet. What can I say? They won't understand. What is there to say? I can send a bag of toys between them for Christmas and birthdays. I don't know what kind of life they lead now. Someone else is making all their decisions for them. I can't even think about their life. I'm just worried about them all the time. Mothers should always be with their kids. All my friends have children and I'm not allowed to see or be near them if they are under 16 years. My sister has a young child so I can't see her now. I can't mix with my old friends at all. I've made such a mess of everything." *B. 21, West Hill, Winchester .*

"The Social Services say I can have the kids to visit in prison but I'm dreading it. What can I say? I've never been a proper mother. They shouldn't have seen me do drugs. I don't write to the kids like some of the women. I won't know what to say if I do see them. Some of the women say I will know but I'm not sure." *C. 41, Mother of five, Low Newton.*

"Now I only get to see him for one hour every two or three weeks. It feels like I've had the very air I breathe taken away from me. He is only fourteen months old and I'm missing all these first important steps in his life."

J. 21, HMP Eastwood Park.

"I just regret the mess I've made of it all. I hope and pray that my children don't end up like me. I can only wish that by my mistake they won't do the same and they will be better people."

D. 37, HMP Wolds sentence 12 years served 3 years 2 months. Five children.

Are mothers indispensable to children?

" I thought stupid things like would she love me? What if her periods started and I wasn't there for her? What if she wanted her Dad? I feel the pain still – knowing her Dad left her and then I ended up where I did."
H. 43, mother of one daughter, Low Newton

"From the age of fourteen the only thing I've ever wanted is a baby! I wasn't interested in money or the latest trainers. I just wanted to be a mother and just before I turned fifteen I fell pregnant for the first time. I was so excited and happy but unfortunately I had a miscarriage at five months and over the next three years I suffered losing another three babies. I began to worry I would never carry a baby full term. So when I fell pregnant at nineteen I was obviously worried but I gave birth to a beautiful baby boy and named him Chauncy (my little miracle). From the day Chauncy was born to the day I was arrested I never spent more than a couple of hours away from him and that was only because my Mum would beg me to let her take him shopping with her or spend hours convincing me I wouldn't be a bad mother if I went to the cinema or pub with my friends once in a while. Now I only get to see Chauncy for one hour every two or three weeks. It feels like I've had the very air I breathe taken away from me. Chauncy is only fourteen months old and I'm missing all these first important steps in his life. Sometimes I fear that he is so young that he won't remember who I am when I get out of here. It's not being in prison that is hard – it's being away from my baby. Having the one thing that means everything taken away from me. There's not one single minute that passes when I don't think about Chauncy and for me being a mother in prison is like the world without sunshine. Cold and dark."
J. 21, HMP Eastwood Park her baby is fourteen months old.

Family abroad?

"My life is a nightmare. This is the first time I've been in prison. I have five children from ten to twenty years. Only the ten year old lives in this country. The others are back in Jamaica. They are from different mothers. I've lived here since 1997 but I've been in prison most of that time. I can't give anybody any advice except tell your children you love them and you'll always be there for them. Because I have a long sentence I can't think about seeing my family back in Jamaica. I write to them but I don't get many back. It's difficult for them because I am so far away. But then I still felt it was the right thing to do to tell them I was in prison, or where would they think I was all of this time? I get extra 'phone cards so I can ring back home. We arrange a time so they can all be there together and I talk to each of them for a couple of minutes. I just have to accept that there's nothing else I can do.

In my culture most of us had children young. It's what we did. I don't regret that at all. I just regret the mess I've made of it all. I hope and pray that my children don't end up like me. I can only wish that by my mistake they won't do the same and they will be better people. I will maintain our relationship forever. I hope I can go back to Jamaica to see them one day, but it is such a bad place with drugs."
D 37, HMP Wolds. sentence 12 years served 3 years 2 months. Five children.

"I have a little girl, she is two and a half. My wife was five months pregnant when I was arrested. This is the first time I've been in trouble and I got this long sentence (15 years). I went straight to prison on remand. She had only been living in this country for a short while. We had been living in India for one year, I had always lived in this country. She had only been here to visit before she came to live here. She was absolutely distraught when I went away. She lives with my Mam now, who supports her even though she's ill herself. She has been diagnosed with cancer. And I've got a fifteen year sentence. It's too long to even start and think about life with my child. I feel awful that my wife is going through this. How can I ever make this time up to her and my daughter? I worry if anything happens to my Mum while I'm inside. I've lost everything, what can I say? I waited to get married. The child was planned. My business was going well and by being in the wrong place with the wrong people I've ended up in here."
J. 40, HMP Loudham Grange sentenced to 15 years served 2 his daughter is 2¹/2.

"I have been three times to see my mother and travelled from Holland each time. It is very difficult because she is not in our country so I cannot see her every day or so, just once in every two months. I live with my sister and I feel very lonely without Mum. We both miss her very much. I tell some problems to a friend but not all of my friends know where my mother is. To come and see her here is good because I can see then that she is OK. My Aunt told me all that had happened when my mother was arrested, she helps me very much, she is my mother's sister. I work to pay for my visits expenses, one of my employers knows where my mother is, I had to tell him in order for me to work more hours sometimes to get a lot of time away from work to come to England. I still tell my mother any problems that I have, she wants to know, she will always be our mother so it's natural to tell her of any problems. I would tell a friend with parents in prison to keep in touch always and to tell them your problems and how you are feeling about everything because that may help them and help to give their parents the feeling that they are still important in their lives. They are parents and it is still difficult for them to be alone. I hope to be here for the trial, it was supposed to be this week but it is delayed now for three months, I will do all that I can to be here. We, my sister and I have flown here before, my mother

"I still tell my mother any problems that I have, she wants to know, she will always be our mother so it's natural to tell her of any problems."

Mika 21, comes from Holland to visit her mother.

"It gets to me when I know they're out (daughters), who they are mixing with etc. What if anything happens? I'm not there, but then maybe I should have thought of all of this before I ended up here. But you never think it's going to happen do you?"

has been in prison for six months and it is so expensive to fly. We now come here with the boat from Den Hague and the train because it costs less this way. We stay here for four nights in a hotel. When I am home, my mother 'phones three or four times every week and we are always sure to be home for those calls because they are so very important to all of us. My mother came on holiday to England with a boyfriend and he had cocaine, he told the police that my mother knew he was carrying this drug, my mother told us that he was not telling the truth and we hope to show this court that she is not lying, that she is telling the truth. My mother is a very strong person, a good person, and she will be strong as we will until she comes home to our family"

Mika 21, lives in the Netherlands and visits her mother who is remanded in custody in London.

Staying in touch or in control?

"We talk every day on the 'phone. I really feel I'm still very much part of her life and have total involvement in the decisions that go on for her. I think we probably talk more in the time we have together than most families do at home. How many blokes come in from work, have their meal and fall asleep in front of the TV? Well, I don't do that do I? We talk all the time and she tells me what she's doing. I don't think husbands or wives should make decisions on their own. They should talk to each other first. I'm lucky that I can, but I know plenty in here who don't have a clue what is going on out there. I think you have a choice to either work at your relationships or not bother at all. But really, if it's worth anything or actually means anything and there is love there, you shouldn't have to work at it. It should just come naturally. I 'phone my wife and daughter every day. My crimes have helped my family in a way. They've never been short of anything. Money was always available. My wife is great with her and I never have that to worry about. We all look forward to the visit. They always go well, but I think it's because I maintain contact. I'm a good Dad and I know she loves me. My wife understands, she gives me and my daughter time together. What else can I do to be involved? I can't think of anything. I hope to be graded to a prison so that I can get home visits and that will be great, so we can spend proper time together. But I don't want her to stop doing the things she has to just 'cause Dad's home for the day."

W.44, HMP Wolds sentence 10 years, he has served 2 years 6 months, his daughter is 8 years old.

"It gets to me when I know they're out (daughters), who they are mixing with etc What if anything happens? I'm not there, but then maybe I should have thought of all of this before I ended up here. But you never think it's going to happen do

you? When I 'phone I ask what they've done, who they hang around with. I try to help with homework best I can. We talk about school and their friends. It's the only way of keeping contact. You've got to be interested in their lives. They still have to get on with things. Their life can't stop because I'm in here. It's upsetting. I only know what I'm told and that's the awful bit about not having control."
R.42, sentence 9 years served 3. Loudham Grange two daughters aged 14 and 16.

"When I go home I spend time with my baby. I'm watching him grow. It's awful because when I leave he says 'Da's gone'. It's good going home even though it's bad leaving them. I 'phone every day to hear him. When you've got a good relationship with the mother it's easier to keep contact. My daughter from my first relationship is eleven now, she wasn't planned. I was only sixteen and her Mam was only fourteen years. So you can imagine how popular we were. The relationship didn't work, but I had access every weekend from Friday to Sunday for six years, in fact until I came here. But her Mam stopped access earlier in the year. I didn't want her to see me in here. I had a good relationship with her and I'm sure we'll be able to pick it up. It hurts when my family see her in town and hear her say things her Mam has said about me and my family. But she's old enough to remember the good things we did together like horse riding and swimming."
A. 27, HMP Kirklevington Grange, sentence 3 years 6 months. Served 19 months. Daughter of 11 and son of 18 months.

"Blokes should always send their families V.O.'s. It's hard for them to visit but they need to know they are wanted. It's hard to tell them you love them. I don't know if it's harder being a bit older or whether it's helpful. Dads should always remember birthdays and send a card from their cash. I can only suggest parents keep writing and taking an interest in their lives. Keep the contact by writing. It's hard inside but it's harder for the kids on the out, but they can read your letters over again."
E. 46, HMP Kirklevington nine children aged 9 –24.

Keeping in touch and advice to others

"Getting an answerphone was a godsend, I was getting some hate calls and I would only pick up the calls I wanted to, also, the fellas are let out at silly times and if you work you can't always be there when they call. Michael would leave messages for the girls and I put them onto a tape that they could play – a Daddy tape." *Jane 38 , mother of Anne 8 and Mae 6.*

"If I was to give any advice to other people in the same circumstances I would say try to be as supportive as you can - for instance write lots of letters to your family member inside. I know that my wife really appreciates them, as it is their only contact in the outside world."
Stuart 32, father of three – his wife is serving a prison sentence.

"I think it's important to not let the family fall apart - it's not going to be forever so don't let it ruin things in your family 'cos your family is really important."
Claire 15, her Dad was sent to prison.

"I think that you have to try and keep a positive attitude - otherwise you'd just go under. I count us as very lucky as we were able to stay strong enough to stay together."

Elise, 35.

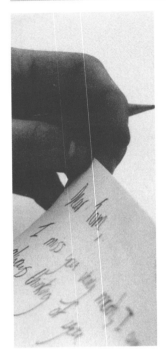

"For me to give advice to somebody else like me I'd say first and foremost don't take any drugs there. My friend's got four kids and I don't know how she does it, she buys her bloke trainers and everything, mind the kids have everything as well, they don't do without, but I wouldn't do that, no luxuries for him mate when I've got my kids to think of." *Lena 25, visiting her partner.*

"I know I was one of the lucky people who had support and love, but nothing will ever take those feelings away from me, even though I was only away a short time. It did feel a lifetime. If I had to do any longer I don't know how I would have coped, so my heart goes out to those parents who are separated for some time. Just don't give up being a parent in whatever small role – it's better than a child not being loved or thinking their parents don't want them." *M. A mother aged 43, who was separated from her daughter aged ten while in Low Newton.*

No privacy

"I didn't even like writing letters because I knew that they could read every word – I knew what he felt about me and he knew what I felt about him and we just had to think on that and not write things down. The 'phone calls were more important, I valued them but he couldn't always talk on the 'phone – it's bad enough that you can't say what you want on visits, but you can't on the 'phone either." *Elaine 28, mother of three children aged 11, 4 and 2 years.*

"I didn't even like writing letters because I knew that they could read every word – I knew what he felt about me and he knew what I felt about him and we just had to think on that and not write things down."

Remote Control?

"Tommy got a 'phone card and rang me, I was going somewhere in the car and had the music playing, Tommy was going mad, asking where I was and why was I somewhere where music was playing, I had to turn the radio up and down to convince him that I was only in the car. Tommy's uncle has a pub and I went up there once to borrow some money from him, Tommy 'phoned while I was there and he was saying to me what are you doing there? Why are you in the pub? I'll 'phone you at the neighbours house in twenty minutes – that was to make sure I had gone home." *Lucy 34.*

"He is really jealous, his jealousy was a really big problem when he was out. He 'phoned me really early one morning from the prison to check up that I was at home and that nobody else was there, I went berserk and he hasn't done that since. I'm on my own but I can't do my own thing. He doesn't trust me and I don't do anything wrong – it makes me feel like packing it in, if he doesn't change with his jealousy I will pack it in." *Teresa, 24.*

Guilt trips

"They are cocooned in there, he has no concept now on the value of money, he does stupid stuff, fritters it away – like on Saturday he got a Giro and spent £115 on Barbie food for the kids, he was just trying to over-compensate. Then, because of him spending the money I had to cancel my hairdresser's appointment and because I couldn't go he went on a huge guilt trip." *Lucy 34, lives with partner Tommy and her five children.*

Difficult to get to 'phone or get letters

"While I was in Durham I couldn't 'phone often. There's this big queue and you wait and wait and then you're back in your cell and you haven't been able to 'phone. They kept moving me so I was really worried about getting me letters. I was on three different wings in three weeks. It took a week for me letters to reach me. For the length of time I was in there was nowt to do – just books and I don't read. We was locked up 23 hours a day, in the induction wing, it was doing me head in, no air and moving me all the time." *J.32, now released from Durham, lives with his girlfriend and three children (hers) ages 11, 4 and 2.*

Teenagers may want one to one

"When he first got taken away, it was so hard. At first he hadn't accumulated enough money to write to each of us so he just wrote to me. The girls were a bit resentful at first 'cos they wanted to hear from their Dad but they wanted their own letters, they wanted to be able to communicate with him themselves. Everybody wrote to him individually but it was getting the letters back. Once he'd stocked his money up he wrote individually. He didn't want to only send one letter to one of the girls if he couldn't write to both." *Trudi 40, husband served a 22 month prison sentence, two daughters.*

"I wouldn't mind talking about Mum, Nanny, and I can talk for myself, you never let me talk for myself, it's the same when we're with Mum, you always want to do all the talking for me, I wish I could spend some time on my own with Mum." *Natasha 15, lives with her grandmother and visits her mother every month – twice if they can manage it.*

Imaginary contact

"We made a pact with each other that at 9 o'clock each night we would say 'goodnight' to each other and kiss our photograph we both had next to us. I only had one photograph of her next to my bed in the cell. I couldn't put lots up as I felt she was too clean and innocent to be in that environment."
M. 43, Low Newton, daughter of ten.

"We introduced a system, at 7.30 the girls would look out of an open window and so would Michael and they would blow a kiss and say goodnight. The little one would elaborate on this and tell him everything that had happened in her day, we used to say that the kiss fairy must have forgotten some things when Michael couldn't remember a whole week's events. There was a time – 7.30 when we all came together." *Jane 38, 2 children age 8 and 6.*

"My Mum kinda blames herself for the way I am, but I tell her I chose this way."

S.16, Feltham YOI.

"I didn't get to talk to him that much even though I wanted to 'cos Mum wanted to talk to him, although he phoned every night."

Claire 15, visiting her father.

When contact hurts

"I send cards to my little girl and sometimes speak to my son but I don't know what to say. I'm not sure if they know me. Some of the girls here draw pictures and write to their kids all the time but I don't. I feel worse when it's their birthdays or Christmas. I don't know if they would be better off without me? I feel bad and I am a bad mother. I do feel guilty but what can I do? I can't change what happened and I want them to have a better life. I had nobody when I was young – I hated everybody – it's hard to know what to do. I feel that I have let them down. I haven't seen much of the kids since I came in here and I don't know what will happen when I get out. I am a bad mother really as I don't think of them very much."

Mother, Low Newton

"First you have to queue for the 'phone, and you start rehearsing in your head what you're going to say to her. This prison has more telephones than most. Have you ever been on the end of a 'phone line and suddenly you realize you're doing all the talking? You're yacking away and she's saying nothing, because she simply hasn't anything to say to you?"

Taken from 'You feel like a stranger', contributions to Chris, writer in residence, Kirklevington Grange.

"We are the silent victims. I am not saying it's been easy inside, but it's hard out here. When I visit, I go through all kinds of emotions; I'm knackered, elated, frightened about the long journeys on my own. I am emotionally drained."

J. 40, visits her partner in HMP Acklington.

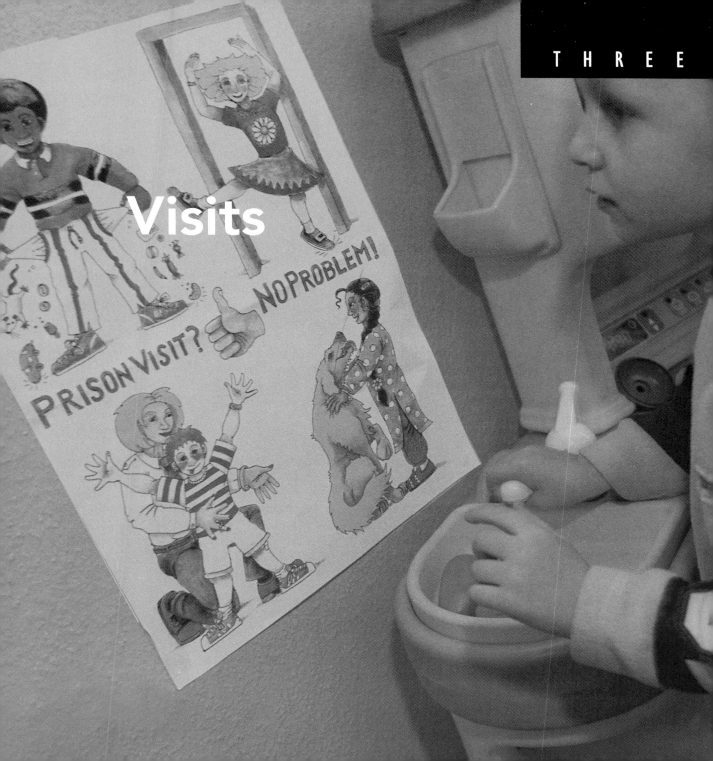

Visits

CHAPTER THREE - VISITS

What makes a good visit?

Tensions and emotions run high on all sides before a visit: Families may have travelled many hours to get there – like the mother and sister who travelled ten hours for a one hour visit. Money and distance worries dominate. Some only find out their relative has been moved the night before a planned visit, and the security searches leave people wound up. Delays in getting the visit started might mean the time together is cut down, raising the tension even higher. Couples report having rows when they finally get to see one another, or forgetting to say what they meant to. Then there is no chance to sort it out until either a 'phone call is possible or the next visit. The visiting relative is torn between wanting to hear their relative inside is OK, and being furious when they hear he has been playing table tennis while she has been battling with three kids, a hot dinner and paying the bills.

The prisoner may be agonizing about putting his child through the security searches, or tense because the visit might be cancelled. He may be jealous about his partner's life outside or hurt that some other man is bringing up his child. Squeezing a relationship into two hours is bound to be hard and parting is painful on all sides.

Conditions and help seem to vary so much from prison to prison. There are visitors' centers in some prisons but not in all, and the type of help available in each varies greatly. Booking systems can be frustrating and impossible to get through to, while others are a model, trying to keep families together. There are still too many people who do not know that they may be eligible to apply for an assisted visit or any other help. People are very private and often feel 'I am not the type to go to agencies'.

On the other hand, rules on who may qualify don't seem to recognise the way many families live today either. Listed at the back of this book are a few agencies or charities to help you and a 'wish list' put together by people taking part in this project.

"This prison is good. They treat us as Dads. I don't know if it's different for the younger lads but I've found it OK. After visits, you can book a photograph with your kids. It works well. They go away with a picture of me to keep me in their minds. Each one has it taken with me. They all want to be the last as that means they have more time with me and get the last cuddle. I treasure the photographs and I know they do." *G 37, three children 9.8 and 6. HMP Wolds.*

"This prison is good. They treat us as Dads. I don't know if it's different for the younger lads but I've found it OK. After visits, you can book a photograph with your kids.
It works well. They go away with a picture of me to keep me in their minds."

G. 37, three children aged 9.8 and 6. HMP Wolds.

"Lichfield held a family day at the prison which I thought was a brilliant idea, I was shown around the prison with my son - it really helped me to understand what it was like for him, helped get rid of the horrible visions of what prisons are like that I had before. You see all these stupid things on TV and frighten yourself to death but it isn't really like that." *Alison, 41.*

"It's the best feeling in the world to have your daughter or your son wrap his arms around you on a visit, specially when you haven't seen them for some time. It's good 'cos although it's only a small amount of time, you still get to bond you know. I look at my daughter when I get a visit and although I haven't been there – I see me, 'cos she looks just like me – and when she comes and wraps her arms around my shoulders it makes up for a lot of things you know and makes me feel when I get out I know what to do. I can sort her out, yeah."
Young father, Swinfen Hall.

"I visit every other week with my sons. They take turns. Then I have a visit on my own. The lads are great when they visit. They have no problem talking with their Dad. They know why he is in. We could not hide it. We didn't want to really. That's not to say I am not ashamed. I'm not proud but we are not the type of people who say 'it wasn't me'. We've taken the blame and we are paying the price."
C. mother of two teenager sons, husband in Acklington serving a 7 year sentence.

"In the last prison I was in before here there was more input for children's visiting. They had a 'playtime' where you could spend time together painting, reading books – doing fun things together rather than sitting on a formal room. It's good to have that time with children and it keeps that bond going."
P. 24, HMP Kirklevington Grange Grange serving a four year sentence, served 2 awaiting decision on parole. His daughter is now four.

"It's going to be different here than at the other prison. It was awful when they came to visit. It's such a long day for them, but it's nearer to home here and the visits are much more relaxed. I'm going to make the most of it. I'll get home visits once a week after I've been here a while. That will give me a chance to get to know them again. I think if cons get the chance to come somewhere like this they should try to. It will be easier in a way as the children get my letters and I can see them at home. I'll have more idea of their life and can take more interest in it. I think it will be best to spend time playing with the kids when I get out once a week."
B. HMP Kirklevington Grange serving 4 years, served 13 months, daughters aged 7 and 6 and a son aged 18 months.

"It's the best feeling in the world to have your daughter or your son wrap his arms around you on a visit, specially when you haven't seen them for some time. It's good 'cos although it's only a small amount of time, you still get to bond you know."

"The tension of the visitors centre is so high you could cut it with a knife. The strain! Taking two buses and the train with small children... trains get delayed or don't run. Getting searched... So degrading and obvious in front of the children."

Mother of two visiting her children's father.

"I didn't take the kids on visits because I wanted to spend the time just with me and him to be able to talk and everything. The little one can't sit still and he would have been running riot in the visits room and I would have had to keep chasing after him and my husband would have got all wound up because he couldn't have run after him because the prisoners have to sit on their own seat and not get up off it. It would have just wound my husband up. If he had been away longer I would have had to take the kids on visits but as it was only for a few weeks I didn't think it really mattered that much."
Laura 23, mother of two sons aged 5 and 3 years.

"It's really good for the kids there, they have a lovely play area and lots of toys and things for them. The visitors' block is good too."
C 25, takes 18 month old toddler.

"The girls were very good on visits because of the crèche facility, I made it an adventure, bribed them with sweets, they would make a long mental list of things to tell him, I resented them being there, I had to take a back seat, I felt cheated."
Jane 38, mother of Anne 8 and Mae 6.

"The staff are always really nice to us when we go to visit, they fuss over the baby. I've never had a problem with visits or things, the staff are fine with us, they've searched Claire's pockets and things but nothing too bad, they don't get too close to her or anything."
Christina 25, partner is remanded in custody, their baby is three weeks old.

"The women at the visitors' centre were helpful and gave me a leaflet."
Teresa 24, visiting her partner in prison for the first time.

"I usually drive to the jail and take both the children, unless that is the older one has something better to do you know like swimming or the cinema or something. He (partner) understands that and thinks the boy should be doing nicer things than going to the prison." *Lena 25, mother of 7 year old and six month old sons.*

"I came to terms with it more when he was in Stoke Heath as I was relaxed in visiting him there cos they were so friendly, they put you at ease, no nastiness or bullying during the searches, it was though you were going into a big supermarket, something you did every week, which I did do every week, they would say "oh he's still here, we'll let him out soon." That helped me come to terms with it. I realised that with all the things he was doing, they turned him around with the education which he'd never done before. Once I could see he was settling then I could settle. His sister had the approach, it got to a point where we enjoyed a Saturday cos we knew we were going to see him. That's

when we got rid of the embarrassment 'cos you realised that the people who were there were the same as you, so you hadn't got to put a face on as everyone was in the same boat. Once the family was told and there were a few tears, that was it and it was finished, after that I began to see another side of it, why he went to prison and why others do as well as it turned my life around as well."
Lorraine 45, visiting her son.

Information – "You're up against a brick wall."

Immediately after sentencing, families lack information on how to find out where their relative is being sent or held, what they are allowed to bring for prisoners, and how to set up visits. Some do not know for days where their child or partner is. (Read about Jeannie in the young offenders section). Few know about 'phone card arrangements, or bringing clothing, toiletries or money to their relative. Rules can apply to children under sixteen who must be accompanied by an adult, and cannot see their parent alone. First visits are traumatic as babies' bottles and nappies are searched, sniffer dogs can terrify, and delays are commonplace. Having someone go with you the first time would help, especially to keep a small child occupied. Small change and more than one form of ID are needed. Later on, prisoners are often moved suddenly and relatives may be planning a visit to the old location. The lack of information is summed up by a comment in a visitors centre comment book:

"Communication: zero. Confusion: 100%."

"It's so important to get more information - I still don't fully understand what's going on - what you can or can't do. You are so lost when this all happens and lack of information just adds to that pressure. You dread the visit the first time - you need someone there to befriend you, support you and explain what is going on, what you should do…" *Alison 41, visits her son.*

"Nobody explains what to do when you visit and you are in a state of shock anyway." *C. visiting husband in Acklington.*

"Later you know that you have to have change for the lockers and for the machines to get chocolate and drinks from. You don't know anything at first, but even the roughest people help you. But they didn't even have a visitors' centre there then." *Jeannie, visiting son 15.*

"I know that compared to some people, having your husband sent away for six weeks doesn't seem like a lot, but it felt like a long time to me. I had never been to a prison before, never visited anybody and I rang Durham prison for information on how to get there and about visits and things and they were totally unhelpful and couldn't even be bothered to give me the proper details to

"It's so important to get more information - I still don't fully understand what's going on - what you can or can't do. You are so lost when this all happens and lack of information just adds to that pressure."

Alison 41, visits her son.

write to him or anything, no explanation about visits, nothing. When he got moved to Wetherby there was no information then either but at least I was a bit more used to it by then."
Laura 23, she had never visited a prison until her husband was sentenced to three months.

"When he was moved from Durham to Wealstun I was left for two days not knowing and worrying where he was, I rang the jail and they would tell me nothing – why couldn't they have just called me and said 'we're shipping him out to Wealstun? That would have saved me two days of worrying, I was on his details as being next of kin – I really can't understand why they have to treat us like shite – they point blank refused to tell me anything. The only thing I knew was that he had gone from Durham because I rang on the Monday to book a visit for the Tuesday and they told me that I couldn't book a visit because he wasn't there."
Elaine 28, visiting her husband who was serving a six month sentence.

"The only thing I knew was that he had gone from Durham because I rang on the Monday to book a visit for the Tuesday and they told me that I couldn't book a visit because he wasn't there."

Elaine 28, visiting her husband who was serving a six month sentence.

"Basically I didn't have anyone telling me what happened next, the solicitor told me where Paul had been taken to and I just had to go home and get on with it. I have a good friend and my family have been good but frankly, you get no information and no support from the system. The solicitor told me that I could go to the prison the next day and be allowed to see him, I went down there, fortunately we live very near to the prison, I asked them face to face for information and they did explain things – that I needed a VO and that they didn't do reception visits – I was literally up against a brick wall, I was disappointed, I was in shock, my head was already in bits trying to take it all in." *Jackie 37, taking care of her three children when her husband is sent to prison for the first time.*

"The visits centre staff were very helpful, but it's that feeling that everyone's watching you, I used to do it myself in the end." *Jane 38, visiting her husband.*

"The first time we went to visit he was in a right state. he hadn't had a shower, he didn't have any clean clothes. Nobody informs you, or lets you know to bring any. Then when we did take his clothes up we had to fill out a form. We were told it was too late and he still couldn't have his clothes until the next visit.It's nobody's job to let you know and he didn't have a phone card." *Shirley.*

"Malka at the visitors centre was very helpful but other than that I got no support at all, you'd pick up leaflets and things that were lying around but none of them were any good."
Lucy 34, her partner has been sentenced for the first time.

"There wasn't any information - I feel left out in the cold about everything."
Jill 47, her son is serving a prison sentence.

"I didn't know what I was going to do. When my husband was arrested the kids were hysterical - I rang a friend and had them taken away to stay with them. I kept 'phoning the station to try and find out what was going on, what was happening to my husband but I couldn't get any answers. I then had to go to the police station to make a statement and the house was searched."
Elise 35.

"If there was someone there to explain things to you, it might be better. Even the barristers don't say nothing. They certainly don't say anything after the court case. The barrister just said that he was going downstairs to talk to my son and off he went. They should have said as soon as they know where he was going I'll be told, but I didn't even know where they had taken him."
Jean 45, son served a prison sentence.

"To be honest the way the justice system works, you just float through it, there's nobody there to help you. I was lucky in that I found a leaflet for SHARP who were brilliant and explained all the procedures - what was going to happen next - before that I was on my own. No-one sits down and explains anything, the families don't get nothing."
Trudi 40, whose husband served a prison sentence.

"It all started when my son went to crown court, he was sentenced to 2 years and then just taken away, I was totally devastated, we didn't know who to speak to, we were completely in the dark."
Alison.

Visit problems: emotions and partings
"Sometimes it's hard when we argue and we can't make up until next time I see her. I use 9 twenty minute 'phone cards every week."
D. 20, HMP YOI Brinsford (he has a daughter of three and is with the child's mother).

> **"Children are much better at expressing themselves. They say what they think. Sometimes it upsets me when they ask 'Why can't you pick me up from school Dad?' It's the things you take for granted that you miss."**
>
> *D. 28, HMP Holme House.*

Children

"When she (his daughter) visits it's funny – she is very shy to start with, then she opens up. It's awful saying Goodbye, but it really does break your heart."
M.25, HMP Loudham Grange sentence 8 years served four. Daughter aged 4.

"I didn't see my Dad until about six months after he'd gone to prison. Walking off from him after the visit was the hardest thing. Really, being there was nice, walking in was all right." *K. 16, daughter, visiting her father.*

"The youngest one doesn't understand why mummy can't come home with us, she gets really upset about it. The visits aren't too bad - the children have been searched quite a few times. The visits with her are good but leaving is always very difficult. My youngest child was in tears the first few times, she is gradually getting better at it though now. The children get quite scared of the sniffer dogs." *Stuart 32, supporting his wife through her prison sentence.*

"There's no sweet machines and they are bringing children and you feel really sorry for them. You can sometimes get sweets and chocolate but you can't get a sandwich, something decent to eat. There's no facilities for heating bowls, so you can't even take it in, so why can't they have some baby food in there? If it is only for the kids, they are being dragged by Mum, auntie, Nan or whoever is taking them there and they go all that way and the poor little sods are starving! A bar of chocolate or crisps isn't healthy and when they have got to go all the way back they really haven't got the inclination to stop on the way back either."
Trudi 40, husband was sentenced to 22 months.

"I hope to go to a Cat C prison next year and I hope things will be better for visiting. I don't like them (daughters aged 14 and 16) coming here. The security is so tight. Once my eldest came. She had made an effort to put her hair up nice, but she was asked to take it down to check for drugs. I've done wrong, but they don't need to go through all that. That's why I don't want them to visit, much as I want to see them. It is upsetting - even the hardest man gets choked at visits. It's awful when they go. All through the visit you think of the time you have together. I try to be a Dad to them." *R.42, sentence 9 years, served 3. Loudham Grange two daughters aged 14 and 16.*

"It's very hard for him on visits though because she's at that age where she's just really found her feet and she wants to run around a lot. She wants Shaun to play catch and chase with her and he's not allowed to move off his seat, it's horrid, Claire gets upset. He's not even allowed to have any of the baby's drawings and things, they have a play area there at the prison but he's not allowed to go and

see what she's doing in there, she does her little paintings for him and he can't take them from her. We always bring them home and post them to him, but to her it must be like her Daddy doesn't want her drawings, It's horrid."
Janet 21, her partner is serving 2¹/₂ years their bay is 18 months.

"The visiting could be hard, I got searched quite a lot, that was probably the worst thing about visiting - I had to put all my stuff in a locker as you can't take anything in with you. I found it frightening. It was really weird seeing Dad in prison. They had all these round tables, it was really crowded and noisy with 3 or 4 prison officers." *Claire 15, on visiting her father in prison.*

That first visit

"I saw your flyer in Art class and had to write a.s.a.p. as I felt it applied to me so much. I'm currently on remand and was in Belmarsh for the first two months. It's quite sad really that I was only going to be at my daughter's side when she was very ill and drove dangerously. I sent a V.O. to my partner and daughter aged 8. When I found out they booked a visit I was so so scared and running with all types of emotions. My problem was first – how should I be on my visit to make it as least painful as possible? I thought if I go on the visit positive and happy, my daughter may grow up thinking jail can't be bad as Dad is OK, and thus be no deterrent for her. Second, I thought I would go out there being sad and unhappy. Then thought it would be horrible for my daughter to see her father like this and make her cry and sad. I felt trapped in a no-go Catch 22 situation. As the first visit day came I said to myself – just be yourself – forget about every thing going on around you and prison officers and be as positive as possible about the future. I did this and it was an amazing visit even though I cried when they left, in front of 150 prisoners. I thought they would belittle me for this as so much is expected from you as a 'Big Man' in jail. The opposite happened and I was comforted by a murderer, he spoke to me and I felt 100 times better. I have not seen my father for 25 years now and feel bad and that I've lost out just as she is now." He adds: "I have no problem for you to use my info in any way that may help others." *A. is at HMP Chelmsford. His daughter is 8 years old. A. lost his first daughter to meningitis. His second daughter developed a high fever and her father panicked and drove dangerously injuring a police officer while trying to get to her. He is particularly concerned to keep his relationship with her.*

"The first visit was the hardest - me and my husband were both trying to be brave for each other, but inside I was worried about everything Once you've been once it does get a bit easier. I had a lot of trouble getting used to being searched, I found it really frightening. I always said that I wouldn't cry during the visit 'cos I wanted to try and act brave in front of him." *Elise 35, visiting her husband.*

"When I went to visit I remember seeing this woman's baby get searched, the baby's juice got searched. My niece went to visit my brother once but I wouldn't want my child to go into a prison, I think it's too daunting for them."

Kerrie 24, visiting her brother in prison.

"When I went to see my brother I was frightened to death, it really was a frightening experience. I hated being searched like I had done something wrong. I felt embarrassed and humiliated by the whole experience."

Kerrie 24, her brother was serving a prison sentence.

"I think that Stoke Heath is OK as a prison. I didn't like Brinsford, it was really scary. All the inmates are shouting at you, it was so daunting, I felt like just turning around and going back out again. It made me feel like I was in there. Visiting was a whole different world, it was funny though, 'cos after a while I realised that so many of the people were like us and I think that helped me to come to terms with it a bit. I got used to visiting him a bit after a while."
Kerrie 24, her brother was serving a prison sentence.

Made to feel like a criminal

"People think that if you have a son in prison you should look a mess, that you shouldn't wear smart clothes or something. The officers sent me through the wrong door once, thinking I was doing a legal visit. There was a solicitor in there with me and when he (the solicitor) realized I was visiting my son, he stopped smiling at me, looked right down his nose at me, then turned his back. The prison officer leaned right over the top of me and looked at me as if I was muck. All I wanted to do was work with the prison and have my son re-habilitated."
M. who visited her son during his sentence. He is now released.

"Going in isn't easy, I feel like the criminal, I have to take off my shoes and socks, I have arthritis and it's hard for me to bend down, I've started to wear shoes that come off easy. We know that they have a job to do but they could be nicer about it we know that they must get fed up with their jobs but so do shopkeepers and they still have to be nice. We can't choose to visit somewhere else though can we? It was very difficult to overcome at first but it was the only way to see him."
Louise who visits her son P. aged 24.

"I found the visits degrading, frightening, humiliating. But we did expect that they had to do the searches, as there are a lot of drugs going into prison. I mean I couldn't do something like that, I couldn't risk myself, I couldn't risk him. I was worried that other people in the prison might make him get me to bring stuff in. That was a worry, I had to really sit down and think about that one, lots of sleepless nights thinking well what if he did get in that situation and I'd have to refuse. Most of the visits are midday, so by the time you've had to travel, imagine someone who's got no transport and has to get buses and trains and they finally get there and all they've got is a coffee machine. Sometimes there aren't even enough chairs, we had to take turns in sitting on the bar, which is ridiculous, there were spare seats but they wouldn't let us have them."
Trudi 40, visiting her husband who served a 22 month sentence.

"For me it's a difficult system to battle with, my husband works shifts and he has to drive us, I have to find out when school holidays are, then write to Mick and sort it all out, it's hard to fit it all in." *Alice takes her grandson Lee to see his father who is not her son and not with Lee's Mum (Alice's daughter). She has to organize it with several people first.*

"Each place is different. The checks are different. At Durham the staff in the visitors centre always ask if it is the first visit - really helpful, and lovely with the baby. You just have to get on with it don't you? When the baby was born, he didn't want me to take him in as it is not the place to be, but then he was on remand. I could just go in one day and I didn't have anyone to look after the baby, so I just took him. My boyfriend was mad at me for taking him but since then he has wanted to see him every time I go in. He thinks, like me, because he is too young to know what is going on it's OK for me to take him in, but if he was any older, he wouldn't want it. Visits do wear you out. I hate going. Sometimes on the train, people will ask where are you going? What do you say? I feel stupid when people look at me. They look at you funny when you say where you are going. What do you say? The centres are not the best places and they are always so full and noisy. I hate waiting for my number to be called out. But how else can they do it?"
S. she is 18 years old now, the baby is 7 months. Partner 21, is in HMP Durham.

"The prison knew I was in hospital for an operation on my back, so they made arrangements for 'phone calls to be taken from his credits. But the most humiliating thing happened when I went to visit him. The staff had to take the dressing off my wound just to check I wasn't carrying any drugs. What is this saying? I feel so resentful. If other partners or family say they do not feel resentment they are lying."
Carla, Husband on a 7 year sentence in Acklington.

"It's difficult on visits as I need to talk to my girlfriend, but I need to talk to the kids and have them on my knee. I look forward to seeing them on visits but it's awful what they have to go through. It's done me good talking like this to someone else other than my girlfriend as I don't want to worry her more than she is, but it is a big worry."
B. 26, HMP Kirklevington Grange, has three children ages 7, 6, and 18 months.

"I'm doing this interview for all the kids that sit in the visitor centre. I want them to know they are not crap just because of what their Dad or Mum has done."
Zoe 40, visiting HMP Acklington

"Most of the visits are midday, so by the time you've had to travel, imagine someone who's got no transport and has to get buses and trains and they finally get there and all they've got is a coffee machine."

"I hated going to see him at Blakenhurst - absolutely detested it - it's a hellhole. You have to wait for hours sometimes, trying to get through the different check points, waiting in different rooms before the next check point, you have to go through so many doors, there's just so much waiting around it's horrible. Just to have a 1 hour visit can take all day when you include the travel etc."

Searches, Delays and dogs.

"I hated going to see him at Blakenhurst - absolutely detested it - it's a hellhole. You have to wait for hours sometimes trying to get through the different check points, waiting in different rooms before the next check point, you have to go through so many doors, there's just so much waiting around it's horrible. Just to have a 1 hour visit can take all day when you include the travel etc. I try not to take the kids, I can't bear to put them through all the searches, they still want to go though. It must be awful for parents with smaller kids as there is nowhere for them to play. The sniffer dogs loved me - I've been stopped on numerous occasions by them, they've never found anything on me. But then you either have to have a private visit through glass or go home. I have refused these closed visits as this is the most precious time of the week for me and I don't want to have to sit behind glass so I've just gone home. I don't touch drugs but even if I did I wouldn't risk taking them into prison and getting a sentence myself, things are already hard enough. I think that the being sniffed by the dogs is an unfair procedure to go through, as it never seems to be accurate. They even searched the kids a few times." *Angie 27, visiting her partner.*

"I went through hell going on visits, once, an officer was going over me with a hand held beeper and it kept beeping over my back, he kept saying 'what's that?' my bra strap had turned round and in the end I had to say 'you can look if you want' – In Durham they looked at me as if I was shit on the carpet, in Wealstun they didn't even look at you. I always felt like I'd done something wrong, he was only in there for driving offences – nothing major, my hands sweated so much that they couldn't scan properly and I once had the drugs dog standing with it's nose right at my bum and my hands were sweating more.

It takes for ever to get through the searches and I understand that they have to think about security problems but the searches are awful, they put their hands down your waistband and I once went there with low waisted jeans on and she had her hands right down my front, on top of that I had a denim shirt on with studs down the front and the metal detector was going beep beep beep and my heart was going bump bump bump because you just don't know what they are going to do to you. I hadn't thought about those things – I just wanted to look nice for him but the next time I went I wore high waisted trousers.

You need to have a very strong relationship to cope with this kind of thing, some women seem to be able to walk in and out of there as if they were going for their shopping, I hated it, I wouldn't not have gone because of how I feel about John, I could do anything for him, we have a strong relationship but it's hard when they (staff) can't treat you like you are human beings." *Elaine 28.*

"At first it made me feel awful. I used to think who the hell's seeing me go in here. One day I took my other son with me, he took his passport, but he was refused entry into the prison, 'cos his passport wasn't good enough. I thought well, you can get out of the country with a passport but you can't get into a prison! My wife couldn't visit for around 2 or 3 months. When he was on remand I visited him every day, but it was a terrible feeling, standing outside waiting to go into the prison, and then you're searched, you think 'God what the hell's goin on here.' When he moved prison after his sentence, it used to take me just under an hour to get to the prison and then it would sometimes take me over an hour to get in to see him. Once you were in it wasn't bad. They put him in closed visits for three months after his girlfriend visited him but I didn't know why, which was bad, seeing him behind glass. He then was transferred another few times 'cos of his diabetes as they didn't have the facilities. This meant he kept having to do induction again. The visiting facilities at the third prison were excellent, much more private, visitors centres treated you with respect. They tried to make it like a bit of a home for you. I think they helped him a lot." *Ken 65, visited his son.*

"You are all waiting in one room before the visits, the tension is so high and one girl smokes. The officer says if you don't hand over your lighter none of you will get a visit. You pray silently that she'll hand over the lighter. You worry about your family that have come all that way, spent all that money and might not even get too see you because of something someone else has done. The tension builds up in the visitors too because they've come all this way and they've been kept waiting. Kids might be whining and tired. Finally, when you do get together, tension is so high people argue. 'I've come all this way' etc and the other one says 'Well it's no fun in here either' so the visit starts off wrong. On the way out the mothers try not to cry in front of their children. They may have had such high hopes for this visit." *Jess, now released but formerly in Holloway.*

Sniffer dogs picking up prescribed drugs

"I managed to form a good relationship with my Doctor. He was so understanding, I was really upset that the sniffer dogs kept picking me out. He wrote a list of everything thing that he had prescribed me and I went with it to Blakenhurst at one of my visits. Some of them were on their list as banned, it was so humiliating as I had to talk to them about it in front of everyone. In a way it's quite funny as the prison sees some of my ordinary tablets as highly dodgy!" *Elise 35.*

"The searches were dreadful. I was searched with a dog during one visit and suddenly was being taken away for supposedly class A drugs. I was in shock. I was then taken to a room and strip searched and promptly arrested. They put my arms behind my back. I was so stressed. I was crying. I've never touched drugs. I thought they were going to put me in a cell. I felt humiliated, the handcuffs were chafing my hands. I was put into a van with other visitors who'd been arrested that day. After this horriffic experience it has taken me four months and medication to build up courage to go back again and see my son." *Mary, 42.*

"The staff in Lowestoft were very helpful and pleasant though, not like the other two prisons. It's a terrible experience going somewhere like that and the officers need more training."

"Finally, when you do get together, tension is so high, you argue."

We don't count

"There is no support, the attitude of staff is so awful – their lack of concern about families and where prisoners are sent to, the distances! I'm not the type to join groups. They don't give a damn – don't reply to letters. The staff in Lowestoft were very helpful and pleasant though, not like the other two prisons. It's a terrible experience going somewhere like that and the officers need more training. I once heard an officer yell out at a very young girl who had come for her first visit, she was obviously unsure and afraid, I got up out of my seat and told him off for speaking to the young lady like that, he looked so shocked that I had spoken out. Even volunteers are even sometimes very bad mannered, who do they think they are? I once asked a volunteer on the canteen – 'Why do you do it? Why don't you let someone with a better heart do this?' No one pulls them up because they are too embarrassed, they don't have the confidence and they are scared of the consequences, life has ground them down so badly."
Lorna 54, visiting her son Owen 28.

"They're really lackadaisical there as well, you can wait ages for the visit, I don't know why they don't start taking the tickets sooner so that you can get the full time for the visit." *Teresa 24, visiting partner serving 3 years.*

"I had no problems 'phoning to book the visits but for anybody who has to travel the visiting times are useless, they are not organised to fit in with people's lives. If you have kids to take to school you can't make the 9.30 morning one – not unless you get there late and who wants to do that? You don't want to waste a minute of your visit and if you go for the afternoon one it's impossible to pick kids up from school." *Elaine 28, partner serving a 6 month sentence.*

Prisoners moved far away from family, accumulated visits not happening.

"He's now been moved to Durham, which is too far to travel, and I can't afford it, so I don't really get to see him. It costs £60 in petrol money. He was meant to come back to Blakenhurst for accumulated visits because I can't go to Durham, but I actually only got half the visits I was meant to have because of some confusion. I've just had so many diabolical problems with visits particularly with Blakenhurst, so many of the visits were cut short and it takes so long to actually get to see the person you are meant to be visiting. I didn't mind Frankland Prison as much - they have more set procedures there which makes the visit run smoother - which was much better. One of the hardest things is having to leave him after the visit, it's just so hard to walk away from him - I just want to put him in my pocket and take him home! The actual visits can be hard as well, for example it can get quite embarrassing for the kids to see all the couples all over each other, you don't know quite where to look, you'd be amazed at what some people actually get up to!" *Angie 27, visiting her partner.*

"The prison moved him last week. It was a Friday. They didn't tell me. I was going in the next day. He rang me at 8 o'clock on the Friday night. That's how I found out. I'm sure prisons just do that. I think they see it as part of the punishment. But it has made me and the baby suffer more. It's further to go than Durham. I have to depend on my father to take me in his car every two weeks when I could get a train to Durham. It was easy going to Durham with a baby, there were shops and places to feed him. Out in Cumbria it is just fields. He doesn't like the long car journey, we are all worn out after the visit. I don't get any help towards the cost of visiting. Nobody told me what to do or if I could. But it's better visiting in this place, in one way, the seats are better and we can sit together. The seats in Durham are awful, they are stupid."
S. She is 18 years old now, the baby is 7 months. Partner is in HMP Durham.

"He was in Leeds before and it was easier to visit there because I live near Bradford but he kept kicking off in there, fighting and kicking up, they get fed up with him and they ship him to places like this (Bullingdon), they always move him round because of his kicking off, nobody wants to put up with him. They think they are getting to him by sending him to places like this, but it's not him they make the problems for, because he's in jail isn't he and jail is jail, one is much the same as the next. It's me that they make problems for, it's me who has to travel miles."
Julia 26, visiting her boyfriend.

"We live on the Isle of Wight and this is very hard on us all, Paula has been in three different prisons over the last year, one of them up in Newcastle, it might as well have been in another country for us getting there. I had to make a choice between my daughter and the children, well, the children's education because it took a three day trip to see her up there and I couldn't go on weekends then because I used to work."
Geraldine, trying to keep her grandchildren in touch with their mother.

"I've told him that I'm doing no more visits, it's doing my head in, it's the distance, the hassle, the waiting, it's all just a long drag, he's accepted that, he just said 'whatever's best.' We'll just have to keep in touch with letters and 'phone calls."
Teresa 24, keeping contact with her partner who is serving three years.

"It's the waiting, the waiting. I wait for the buses to get here, I wait here for hours (visitors centre), I wait in the visits room and I wait for him to come home. I'm always just waiting for things."

"He went straight onto advanced and moved to Hewell Grange which is an open prison - this was such a long way to drive. But even though I was severely ill I went every Sunday. He then got some town visits, which were brilliant, but they were long and hard at the same time. My husband agrees that it is much harder for the family than it was for him through the whole experience."
Elise 35.

"They actually took him to a local prison first which was full, then to Stoke which was also full so they then took him to Liverpool which is a damn long way. I don't mind going once a week. My sister takes me, as my car wouldn't make it. I'll get another car if I can afford one after I've paid off my son's debts."
Jean 45, visiting her son of 21.

Booking visits – 'as easy as winning lotto!'

"He's been in most prisons in the country and its always the same system, you keep trying to call to book a visit and they never answer or you are told that they're putting you on hold and then they cut you off, it can take days to get a visit booked, it's a pain."
Julia 26, visiting her boyfriend.

"I can 'phone here for three days trying to book visits, you get put on hold or they don't answer and we can never give the school any notice about taking them out to visit if we can't get a visiting space on a weekend because it's so hard for me to get through on the 'phone and the bills cost loads."
Geraldine, mother of Paula serving ten years, taking care of Paula's two children.

"Booking the visits is a nightmare, the hours I work don't usually fit in with the booking times and when I can 'phone the odd time the lines are nearly always engaged and that's irritating." *Teresa 24, supporting her partner.*

"Trying to book a visit the first time was a nightmare.
I pulled my chair up to the phone at 8.30am and sat there continually ringing until 3pm trying to book a visit. I didn't move apart from to go to the toilet, it was hell."

Jean 45, visiting her son 21

The process impacts on the relationship

"The staff make the visits so frustrating for you as they are rude and unhelpful - they wouldn't advance book visits and I have ended up having loads of rows with my partner because of it - you just don't need the extra pressure or hassles with that." *Angie, 27.*

"I stopped bringing my little boy in here. He's only four and the screws made him stand with his hands in the air to search him like he was scum. My husband's out next week. If he wasn't, he just wouldn't get to see Jake because I wouldn't bring him here again."
Mother, anon.

" I saw a little boy there, he was only about three and an officer had about three fingers in his mouth – checking it, I couldn't have put my kids through that."
Elaine 28, mother of three children.

"My Grandson here is only eight weeks old. My son is doing five years. Nicola (sons' girlfriend) is only 18, she needs a lot of support. I want my son to bond with his baby. He's in there for five years, how will he ever know his child and his child know him? We come here as much as we can, but it's a long way. After all the waiting around we only have half an hour for a visit, how can he bond with his baby when he only gets to hold him for half an hour every now and then?"
Grandmother.

"When inmates get angry with something that's happened in the prison that day, they tend to take it out on those outside; then it makes it worse for them on the out as they don't know what's going on."
P. 24, HMP Kirklevington Grange Grange. Girlfriend and their daughter of 4 years old on the outside.

"If there's no crèche it's an awful visit and the visit depends on your relationship, whether you're there out of duty or if you really want to be there. It was well over a week before I saw him, I went up there by myself and emotions were running extremely high."
Jane 38, husband remanded in custody.

"The only bad thing for me is that the visitors centre closes at 4.45 and we can't get the bus 'til 5.30 so you have to stand the whole time in the bus shelter and it gets so cold at times."

Christina 25, taking 3 week old daughter Claire to see her Dad.

"At Durham I was so uncomfortable that it wasn't worth me going, I felt so bad that there was no proper conversation. It was more relaxed at Wealstun but in Durham the staff would keep walking past you the whole time, they would stop next to you and listen, it's personal, it's not very nice, you've missed them and want to tell them what's going on but you can't even have any private conversation."

Elaine 28, whose partner John was sentenced to 6 months.

"I was visiting him alone most of the time, I told my wife that she'd never cope with seeing him at the second prison, 'cos the process is too bad, waiting in there nearly an hour, then you're searched and then you can be waiting there for half and hour, then you even have to wait in the visiting room up to 30 minutes whilst they call them down, then 30 minutes to get out of there. But in the end she used to ask me how he was all the time, did he look bad? She did feel she could go to Featherstone and she had no quarrels with that, people treated you like an ordinary person. She always had to be one of the first to go in. I didn't like visiting in Shrewsbury, as it's so much stress, it's awful. Blakenhurst I didn't like but maybe it was better than other places, Featherstone was very good to the families. Featherstone was good at Christmas, sweets for the children, more relaxed."

Ken 65, his son was in prison.

Visit or send money?

"I have been without visits now for 3 months as it is so far to travel. This thing is taking over my life. I have to make difficult choices such as if I send him money, which he needs for phone cards and toiletries etc, then I can't afford to go and see him. One visit costs me £100 in total which includes the petrol, then the kids want to stop on the way and I have to get food for them as it's a long journey, I just can't afford it. I didn't even realise I could get financial help from APVU until recently. While he's been there I'm his only visitor, as his parents can't go as it's too far for them as well. The kids don't really understand how it all works, they keep asking me to get him moved to Blackpool so they can have more adventures and go on the funfair!"

Angie 27.

Worries about visits

"I don't like her being near sex offenders on visits. It upsets me knowing people can do that to a child. I worry if anything should happen out there. I've met some scumbags in jail and it makes me feel sick what they've done. I really look forward to the visits but I feel awful knowing they have all the security to go though and I don't want her to have to do that for much longer."
M.25 HMP Loudham Grange, sentence 8 years served four.
Speaking about his daughter aged 4.

"I've got to take off work for Manchester - we only got a one hour visit and we were away ten hours! Sometimes you feel why I have I bothered? You think he'd put on a happy face – we get the moans and 'You'll do all my forms for me won't you Mum?' He puts on a happy face for his friends."
Jeannie, whose son, 21, has been moved many times, facing several sentences.

"It's horrible when you are stood outside the prison waiting in the rain and they won't let you in, like you aren't human and that's the relative! We are treated like the scum of the earth." *Trudi, 40.*

"I was
frightened
to death
at court -
I just kept
thinking '
I just can't
believe
that that
is my son
standing
there-
what is he
doing
there."

Simple practical steps that could help

"It has to be at weekends though because otherwise I can't go. Well the thing is, visits are from 2 'til 4 and it takes me over an hour to get there and I couldn't get back in time to get my son from school. Sometimes I'm just too knackered to go and those times, like with Christmas, I say the car's broken down or something and don't go, I wouldn't tell him that I just basically wasn't going, but I go most every week anyway." *Lena 25, 'fitting in' visits.*

"If I go to see John at weekends you see they (the prison) make you use up two VO's so you only get one visit a month and it's better to go every two weeks, better for Mary as well, that's all wrong I think."
Jasmine 23, takes her 18 month old daughter Mary to visit Daddy.

"If I could only go for a visit in the evenings…what are you supposed to do if you're trying to keep your job? It's all a struggle, I think it's important to take the baby, he's only just getting to know him but it would help if they'd do evening visits – that would be much better for me."
Lena 25, has two little boys aged seven years and six months.

"It's the booking system - absolutely hopeless."

"It's the way they move him around - if they'd let me know...."

"I didn't know where he'd been taken after he'd been sentenced."

- Information should be given out at court.
- Faster notification of next of kin (especially for young offenders) where the prisoner has been taken.
- Provide clear instructions for first visits - what ID is needed, what can be brought to a reception visit.
- Synchronise times visitors' centre is open with local transport.
- Provide reasonable food such as sandwiches and childrens' food to purchase in visitors centre.
- Provide information on assisted visits at the outset.
- Provide shelter from weather for waiting visitors.

Family change

> "I have learned to be an effective Dad in prison. When I was at home with them things were different. I loved them, but not really loved or appreciated them. I don't think I understood what it was to be a Dad. I was always too busy. I'm starting to be an effective parent."

CHAPTER FOUR - FAMILY CHANGE

What happens when faced with a long sentence?

Letting go and new starts.

"The children live with their mother, but we have split up. I decided to give her the option about the relationship when I was sentenced (10 years). We split up. She remarried again but that didn't work out. It wouldn't work between us now, no matter what. I know that now, but that doesn't stop me loving my kids above all else, does it? We decided (my ex-wife and I) to change the school that our kids attended. The school they go to is better for them – they have no hassle there."
G. 37, HMP Wolds sentence 10 years.

"I'm not with my son's Mum anymore. It was me who decided to end it. I don't know if it was the right thing to do, but I felt that because I had a long time to do, it wasn't fair on her to 'wait' for me. Maybe I was selfish but it was the only way I knew to help me get through my time. Too many men worry about what their women are doing on the out. I just didn't want that. She looks after my son well. My family and friends are good with him. They bring him to see me now I'm not with his Mum."
C. 27, HMP Wolds. His son is three, the sentence is 12 years, he's served 3 and a half years.

"He got seven years for a violent burglary, I couldn't believe it, it took the wind right out of my sails, one of my other sons had been to court with him and when he told me what had happened I felt my legs go from under me. Jack had been on remand for eight months and I'd gone to see him every day, I even visited when I had my slipped disk, my oldest son used to lift me in and out of his van, if he was too busy to take me I'd get the bus and stand up all the way because if I'd sat down I might have got stuck in the seat "
Maureen 66.

"I was frightened to death at court - I just kept thinking ' I just can't believe that is my son standing there - what is he doing there'. I went alone to the court, I didn't know what I was doing, I didn't know what I should do, I had no one to talk to…. I just felt so drained by the whole thing. He got so many years more than I thought he would, when he got his sentence I wanted to shout and scream but I just couldn't."
Alison 41.

Can you get closer to your family while in prison?

G. gave his wife the option when he was sentenced, they split up and she remarried. However that marriage has not lasted. The children, aged 9, 8 and 6 live with their mother and attend a new school.

"My sister brings my kids to see me every month, they live on the other side of the country. My sister is great. It's funny, but coming to prison has made us a closer and better family, not just with my kids but with my parents and sister. I was never close to them when I was at home. The more life developed for me, the less I saw of them. I went my own way, that's just how it was. I've always had a good relationship with my own kids but not with my family.

I was in prison six months before I could even tell my parents where I was. I rang them on Christmas Eve. I was in Dover prison, but they came to see me. The bond was there. They say 'the past is past' and we will move on and be positive about the future.

They are good people. Never in trouble in their life, but yet they will support me, and I'm sure they love me. For all that I'm a Dad, a parent to three kids, I'm still their son. I find that really emotional; I bet you think I'm daft?
I have learned to be an effective Dad in prison. I really look forward to our visits. I get quite excited when I know that their visit is booked. When I was at home with them things were different. I loved them, but not really loved or appreciated them. I don't think I understood what it was to be a Dad. I was always too busy. I'm starting to be an effective parent. I talk to my kids now. Visits are good. We talk, catch up with their lives and have a laugh. We always have plenty to talk about. They all want to sit on my knee. They all want the last cuddle and I want to cuddle them all at the same time.

I phone their Mum once a week to get an update on the kids. They don't know I speak to her. I tell them the school gets in touch with me using emails or faxes. I know the truth would be better but it's the only way I can deal with it. Their school is aware of the situation and I'm sure would help them if needed.
People would think me a hard man for my crime, but it was a way of life. I didn't know what else to do. The more you get into it, the harder it is to get out of it. I think I'm starting to sort myself out, but it is hard. No one out there should think it's easy or glamourous. It's not. I feel everything is destiny. "
G. HMP Wolds 37 years !0 year sentence. Served 3 years 2 months.

" I love my parents more as I've thought about it. They must have been worried not knowing what I was up to."

"If anyone could tell me what I could do to help him, I'd do it... anything at all... but no-one could tell me. Friends have tried to comfort me... but I'm ashamed of me."

"We actually got married in prison, which may sound mad, but she wanted to. We were only 21 years old, but she wanted to, so we did. I've been in prison twice before. We had been together four years before our first child was born. We were delighted."
R. married 21 years, now divorced with two children. HMP Loudham Grange

"My family help me and want me to keep clean and I think I will this time. My Mam and Dad are divorced and both have married again. They are happy and take turns to come and see me even though it's quite a travel. They make the time. It makes me feel guilty that I've caused them pain and worry. I love my parents more as I've thought about it more. They must have been worried not knowing what I was up to or who I was with. I've done some bad things and I'm sorry. I think I can make it better. I'm lucky because they love me and I've learned my lesson. I've been in and out of prison four times so I've missed out on having children. Being here with other women who have kids has made me think I'm better off not having any yet. I would tell other parents to love their kids and be kind and listen to them. I want to be a good mother but it must be hard. I'll know what my kids are up to 'cos I've done it all."
S. 24, Currently in TC unit at Low Newton.

Parents pick up the pieces...and the guilt
"I feel slightly responsible...that I couldn't do anything else for him, I warned him so many times but I just couldn't get through to him. If anyone could tell me what I could do to help him, I'd do it... anything at all... but no-one could tell me. I've avoided so many people, I can't look at people or wave at them like I used to, and we've kept very quiet since it all happened. Friends have tried to comfort me... but I'm ashamed of me. People do know that I've brought him up the best that I can, that thought has helped me." *Jill 47, her son was sent to prison.*

"They've been well brought up, it's drugs. I don't think I could have done anything more, they've always had a good home, warm, well fed. I'd be lost without my wife, she isn't their Mum but she takes me to visit my sons, takes me everywhere. It's hard on her, hard on everybody I suppose. He'd been with his girlfriend for years and they've got that lovely baby, well she's not really a baby she's three. They are his family really but she's had enough, he's had loads of chances and she won't have him back."
Danny has three sons in prison – all through heroin. He is severely disabled but visits all of them; one of his sons is a father.

"This isn't the first time John's been to prison but it's the first time since we've been together. It's very hard with money and everything. I'm very lonely. My parents have been quite supportive, I've moved house since he's been in there, I wanted us to have a fresh start when he gets out and they (parents) helped me to move and with the decorating and everything and they babysit sometimes but I don't go out much because its so hard financially." *Jasmine, her child is 18 months old, her partner is in prison for 22 months due out soon.*

"I was devastated when I found out - he hasn't been brought up to steal. He had a very strict upbringing by myself and his father. This all happened very recently and we are all in shock at the moment. His grandma is taking it particularly hard. We haven't broadcasted it. Things are really tough at the moment. We can't go into the shops in our village as he stole from them. I feel utterly ashamed and humiliated of him." *Jill 47, visiting her son.*

"I believed when I got to court I would go home - after all, I had my daughter to look after, she doesn't see her Dad. I had arranged for her to stay at a school-friend's that night thinking I would never go to prison but that I wouldn't be much use to her. I never told my partner or parents, so when the judge told me my sentence, I just wanted to die. I had let my daughter down. The probation officer had to tell my parents who are so quiet and in their own routine that I thought it would kill them. They looked after her until I came home. I was frightened of what my parents might do. I thought they wouldn't want me for the shame I had put on them." *Diane 43, sentence 45 days Low Newton, one child.*

"At the time my son went to Prison I didn't want anything to do with him. Although I supported him at crown etc, it was like a big golf ball in the back of my throat. When we came out I couldn't handle the embarrassment of it all, I was so annoyed that he had done that to us and brought shame on to us. I couldn't bring myself to see him at the reception visit, my daughter went to see him, I sat on the car park for 2 hours, I just couldn't face it, then I came home. I then wrote him a letter, in which I wrote some really nasty things, how much he'd hurt me, put it all down on paper. He's quite cocky and I thought he would send one back saying that he wasn't bothered, but instead he sent me a lovely letter back saying how sorry he was and I think that made him realise what he'd done and I think that punished him more than going to prison. From then he turned completely round. I went to see him 5 weeks later.

In those 5 weeks I didn't cope very good 'cos I wasn't to see him but I thought it was for the best, up until he went to prison he was someone that had to push everything to the limit and finally he got a prison sentence and I wanted him to

"I've questioned myself over and over if I could have been a better mother. I just don't know, but I think every parent out there could question that of themselves."

know that I was having a prison sentence as well. Yes he wasn't allowed out at night but I was still in Prison and I was the one that couldn't face people. I was the one that was taken to prison, he was told what to do, had a routine, I didn't have a routine but I had to face the newspapers, the family, had to tell people like his Nan and it was awful, the most degrading thing I've ever had to go through." *Lorraine 45.*

"I blamed myself, kept asking myself questions such as 'why didn't I do more to help him, had I been in denial before and just couldn't face up to the reality?"
Alison 41, talking about her son who was in trouble over drugs.

Change – kids don't stand still

"When my children came to visit me here my little girl seemed to be a young woman all of a sudden. I have lost that time of her life. It was so strange. When they came I went to buy a drink for her but she said "No Dad, I can do that myself." She had money in her pocket – could ask in another language. Where has my little girl gone? I can't imagine by the time I get out of here what my oldest children will be like. Will I know them?" *J. 43, HMP Wolds sentence ten years three children two abroad, ages 14 and 13.*

"**If prisoners kick off inside it's usually because of what happens on the outside. We get frustrated because we have no control over what's going on.**"

J.E. 43, HMP Wolds

"My little lad was four months old when I came in. I've missed all the first events in his life and I'll never get them back." *D. 28, HMP Holme House served two years.*

"It's important for them to spend time with each other or my baby's Dad would be a stranger to him when he comes out." *Christina 25, mother of three week old baby boy.*

"But when you go home, you've changed, your wife's changed, the kids have changed. The kids more than anything, they treat you like a stranger." *Johnnie (74)*

Older Father

"I've got four sons and they've all been good lads, no trouble or nothing, all good grafters and I take it hard that Jack gets into bother. My wife says it's my fault because Jack had too much of his own way, she thinks I should have been harder on him. I don't know if I should or shouldn't have, the others are alright; all good grafters and what can you do to a little lad? I couldn't have hit him, I would have hurt him. I did a lot of time in my young days, that's when prison was really hard, you weren't even allowed to sit on your bed during the day. I know that time is easier now but I didn't want my boys going inside. I talked to Jack until I was blue in the face about him getting into trouble, he makes out that he's listening, sits there nodding his head and agrees with everything I say, yes Dad, no Dad, then he's out the door and does as he pleases. I couldn't go to visit him, no I couldn't, I've spent enough time in those places, I've been in jails all over the country. I always told Maureen to tell him I was asking after him." *Johnnie (74)*

Mothers

"I've never had any involvement with this kind of thing before. When my son first went to prison I felt as guilty as him. The prison he is in now is better. He was involved with drugs, which we knew about - we tried to get him off them - but he eventually went back on it again. He left home and everyday we were waiting for the police to call, we knew it would happen eventually, but it was still a shock when it actually did. It hurt very bad finding out what he had done, but he's still my little boy - it has been real turmoil. I have a very close relationship with him, everything but the drugs that is. We are all finally starting to get back on track." *Alison 41.*

"I've questioned myself over and over if I could have been a better mother. I just don't know, but I think every parent out there could question that of themselves. Sometimes things are out of control. Then there were times when I was short tempered with my granddaughter and I felt guilty. She hadn't done anything wrong. We all thought it would be like Bad Girls. I was really worried about how she would be when she came home. In fact we could all cope. But I think it's true when you have children you just have to go on for them and you want to for them. In that way it keeps you safe. If you had nobody depending on you I think it could be worse." *S. Her daughter was given a six month sentence, S. did not even know she was going to court and had to care for a ten year old granddaughter suddenly in an emergency.*

"As a mother you always want to fix things for your kids. I couldn't fix this for him. He had to start taking responsibility. He is 6' 3" and I am 5' 4", yet I had to carry him while he was in prison and I felt the full weight of that. I once went to visit him and they had put him on a closed visit and he wanted me to tackle the prison officer about that. I felt I had to do it even though I didn't want to. It all ended up a right mess with me complaining to the Governor and everything. I was worn out. I once took my sister to visit with me and she was ill for two days afterwards. She said she couldn't have coped with it all. I told her 'you would if it was your son!'" *M. Mother of ex heroin addict who is now aged 24. HMP Wolds.*

"We're a very open family and discuss everything, it's no good being a parent then shunning it, you have to get on with it. We're not the type of parents to say 'our kid wouldn't do that' you have to accept that they can do wrong... your kids! And then get on with it. It's like when they were little, they did things wrong and you have to accept that and sort it out and get on with things, you can't think that they're not your kids anymore. We've brought up four kids and Patrick is the only one who's been in trouble but he's faced up to his crime and taking the punishment for what he did, he'll do his time then when he comes out, hopefully we can put it behind us and move on. You have four kids but they're

"As a mother you always want to fix things for your kids, I couldn't fix this for him."

not all the same are they? They're all individuals. I can only go to see him once a month so that has to keep him going for a while. My hubbie is very supportive, I'd have been lost if it hadn't been for him, he takes over the home when I go to visit. His Dad goes sometimes to visit him on his own because Patrick likes to be able to talk about things with his Dad that he wouldn't be able to talk about with me. It's his commitment to our boy as much as mine, he's very much involved, well he's his Dad! – Couldn't have him shunning it! I need my hubbie, I'm more fortunate than most because he's always been there, I would have lost it if it hadn't been for him. The worst times have been Christmases and suchlike, my grandson's christening and times like that, family times. The family have all stood by Patrick but this is his first time. It was my daughter's idea to take Jake on visits (grandson), he's only a baby and doesn't realise where he's going, I probably would have taken Jake still if he'd been older and knew what was going on, I think my daughter would have still wanted Jake to go, it's good for both of them, It's good that they know each other for Patrick coming home. Everybody's been supportive, the whole family, but it's the first time. If it were a recurring thing people might not stand by him." *Louise, supporting her son Patrick (24) serving a three year sentence.*

Parents can feel guilty towards other children.

"I have been guilty of pushing my other son out as everything has been about the one that is on prison - I was too wrapped up in my own grief I guess he was lucky to have good friends to help him through it. Seeing what his older brother has gone through and what he has put us through has taught him a lot - he wouldn't do anything wrong now and he certainly hates drugs!" *Alison 41.*

Family: Support or stress?

"Prison has only taught me bitterness. I shouldn't be here. My youngest son was arrested with me. He was left in police cells on his own. They talked about putting him into care. It's not his fault he was in my lorry. He has lots of emotional problems. Now he's hyperactive; he takes medication and has to see a psychiatrist. He does not fit into the school. He can only go for half days. This cannot be right. He and my wife live in England my other two are with my elderly parents in Belgium. We were middle class and now have nothing. I can't even start to think about my two children who live with my parents. I have missed out on my kids. I will never get it back. I can't think about seeing them it's too painful." *J. 43, HMP Wolds.*

"I go with his Dad on visits because I don't drive. His Dad moved out you see, he got himself a bit of stuff and left. People can't understand why I still talk to him, but he's my kids' Dad and I think that life's too short not to talk to people. Anyway, if I didn't talk to him I'd have to visit on the bus. I was in a right state at first though, ended up on pills and everything. A good friend told me to ditch the pills and move on and that was good advice. Dave takes me with him to visit because he's in ill health, he has angina and so he gets the petrol money for visits." *Sandra, had three sons in prison, talking about visiting Robbie 25.*

"We were living together at Mum's house before prison. My girlfriend is supported by my Mum and by her Mum but not by Dads. My Dad did not want to know. I was

"My Mom is the world of my life"

anon, Feltham.

in care from the age of ten. Then I got a letter from Mum.
I'll be going to advanced foster parents and I'll get an allowance. I told her father I'd look after her no matter what. It's really scary knowing I have that responsibility." *Chris 16, his baby is due within a few months. Feltham.*

"It's my partner who's in prison, at least he's my partner at the moment but I don't know how long for. There's been so much grief in my relationship with him, not before he went to jail, things were OK then but since he was sent away I've had nothing but problems. I have kids, grown up kids and grandchildren and my kids keep on nagging me to stop visiting and to end my relationship with him. Everyone, even his own family are ashamed of him, mine can not understand why I have stood by him. I'm not getting any younger and we got on really well before he was sent away, part of me wants to stick by him but it's not easy with everybody nagging me the whole while, but I think it's not right to leave somebody rotting in prison on their own, he is a human being although he has done wrong. I don't like what he's done but it can't be undone and everybody needs somebody, you can't just leave somebody in prison without anybody to visit and keep in touch." *Jo, 53.*

Letting Mum take the strain.
3 Young Prison fathers talking in Swinfen Hall.

"If I didn't have my mother, I don't know what I would've done. She has the baby just as much as the mother. She buys the baby everything - you name it, she bought it for the baby. She's got seven grandsons but no grand daughters. I've given her a granddaughter and it's like she's really loving it."

"Mine's basically the same. If I come to a difficulty or something, my Mom's there to help me out. But at first my Mom didn't approve of it see, 'cos I was young and that. I was only fifteen as well. At first she wanted nothing to do with it. But when the baby came, after a few months she came round and I don't know what I'd do without her 'cos now I'm in here."

"I don't keep in contact but my Mom plays that role for me. She collects the baby all the time and she tells me all the information. My Mom does it all for me. Photos, letters, visits."

"My Mam is sorting out her Christmas presents for me. I send my Mam money to help out a little. Mam sends me lots of photos of my little girl and of the home. I'll go back and live with my Mam if I get parole next year. My little girl goes to my Mam's often so they have a bond – a good relationship."
M.25, HMP Loudham Grange sentence 8 years served four. Daughter aged 4 years old.

"My Mom does it all for me, photos, letters, visits."

"I lived with a violent man for twenty three years and I know what it does to you, you think everything's your fault and you have no inclination to think anything about you is good at all."

Young Families trying to be a unit – parents are the key

"I live with my Mum and Dad, they're brilliant. I couldn't cope without them, they help me financially and with Claire. I tried to keep working full time at first, I did it for four months but then I couldn't manage it, I realised it was too much for me. I still work weekends and I see most of my friends during the day. I'm not interested in going out of an evening. My Mum comes with me on visits so that if Claire gets upset my Mum can play with her and keep her occupied and I can have more of a relaxed time with Shaun. I definitely need to take Claire to see Shaun, she needs to know who he is and he needs to see her. I'd be in pieces if I didn't have Mum and Dad; I'd sit in all day and be very lonely." *Janet , 21.*

Dad tries

"I've done four months on remand. It's my third time in jail. I'm looking at five years when I get sentenced. I've missed three Christmases and three birthdays. From when I was young I don't really care about life. Everyone got to go sometime, you only get one chance in life. Don't consider myself to have any future you see what I'm saying? There are people looking to kill me. A miracle has to happen for that not to happen. I feel protected inside by friends, but on the outside I have to look over my shoulder 24/7 you see what I'm saying? South London has always been my home, it's difficult to break away. My Dad knows. I'm going to try to change for my little brother. I will try my hardest. My Mum died when I was twelve. Ever since I've been mad. My Dad supported me, no agency helped. Social workers pulled me out of my family and sent me to a foster home two years after my Mum died. For two years I lost contact with my family. From time to time I got a 'phone call but I was never in and I never contacted them. Everyone visited but I wasn't interested. I've never had any counselling. My foster parents had a fourteen year old daughter she could do no wrong. I had an argument with her and my foster father punched me in the face. I went in the kitchen and took a knife to protect myself. He ran out and called the police and a social worker. I was sent back to my Dad's. I started to get arrested when I was in foster care but it got worse when I went home. The trust in my gang broke down. My three friends inside are like family. Dad always came to the police station when we were arrested, he would bail all of us out. The other Dads came sometimes, but my Dad would always come. I don't talk to prison counsellors. I don't trust them. I don't have any contact with the chaplain. My friends are my counsellors. Dad usually comes by himself because I don't get on with my Stepmum. I'm close to my Dad. I think my grandparents, my little brother and my Dad miss me a lot. It's sad innit for both? I feel more sad for them. They have always been there for me."
B. 17, Feltham YOI Remand.

Grandparents: "We were dropped right in it."

"God help me I can't believe this for my own daughter and those poor little children, my own grandchildren. Timmy told the police that he didn't see Daddy hitting mummy but that she was often screaming and cried and had blood running out of her head and face. He raped her the time before he really beat her up. I have to find £1000 today for my daughter's bail money. I was so upset when I left home that I didn't bring my passport with me so the bank wouldn't give me the whole amount in one go. I have ran around London going to different cash points, using credit cards and other accounts and arranging an overdraft to get the bail money.

The way that my daughter and those children were living was terrible; I have a big bungalow with a huge back garden that they can run around and play in. I hope that we can give the children some stability so that they can begin to heal. I lived with a violent man for twenty three years and I know what it does to you, you think everything's your fault and you have no inclination to think anything about you is good at all. Robert was the nicest person you could ever wish to meet until he had a drink. He had an allergy to drink that made him go berserk. He was already on the run for violent assault when this happened.

Jordan told the police that his Daddy had never hit him, but had only thrown him across the room and cut his head, he lifted his hair back and showed the policeman the scar on his head, it's a faint white line now. I haven't lied to the children, they asked if their mammy would be coming to live with us, and I told them that she would be eventually, but that it might take some time before she can do that. But when they asked if their Daddy would be living with us I told them that we'd have to wait and see. I couldn't tell them then that their Daddy had gone to heaven because she wants to tell them herself. The only thing is that she might not get to see the children for months so I don't know what to do."
Bridget has taken the children to live with her, but has come to the prison as her daughter is to be released on bail.

Alice takes her grandson Lee to visit his father. Lee is ten years old:

"Lee is the only reason I go there because the chap in there is no relation to me, he was a friend of my daughter's and they were really good mates I thought, not girlfriend/boyfriend, and there she was – at 17 – pregnant with Lee. They must have been very good mates for her to get pregnant! Mark (Lee's Dad) split up with my daughter when the little one was only ten months old, but they always had a lot of contact. She is married now and has been for six years but her husband doesn't mind Lee going to see his Dad. In fact they were all mates. She won't let Lee visit except in school holidays, the school knows where Mark is. Lee didn't see his Dad for the first year and I went mad and had a row with her in the

" I feel sorry for that chap. He's watching someone else bring up his child."

end. His mother was a big influence on Lee not going, he used to say he didn't want to go and I almost had to drag him kicking and screaming. A year was a big chunk out of the little one's life and he needed to see his Dad. I do it for both of them. He could have exploded in there - not seeing Lee – and it's ruined this little one's life. They're the spitting image of each other and as soon as they see each other Lee sits on Mark's knee and stays there for the whole visit. Mark 'phones the little one every week and Lee says he's glad that he only sees his Dad in the holidays because he wouldn't have anything to tell him with him 'phoning every week. We had to be careful how we told him, but Lee knows what his Dad's in for, we wanted him to know what he'd done wrong and why he was in there. His other grandparents wanted to take him but I think my daughter went over the top with them when it all first happened and the boy won't go with them. I think I got Lee to agree to go by telling him that his Dad was ever so upset about not seeing you and you must go. For me it's a difficult system to battle with. I feel sorry for that chap in there, I do it for him as much as Lee, he's watching someone else bringing up his child. I feel sorry for Mark's parents. They're good people and were ready to move a thousand miles away they were so ashamed. His Dad cried to me just last week. It hits everybody doesn't it? Mark was a great old boy to me, always helped me out, my heart and my prayers are with him in there. He was a good chap."

Maria: Three of my children are addicts.

"Out of my five kids there is only my eldest and youngest daughter who are not now or ever have been addicts. I've often sat back and thought about it all, I've read books about addictive personalities and wondered if that's the reason they went the way they did or are they just weak and can't say no? I am addicted to cigarettes, I know that and their father was addicted to gambling, but he gave up gambling and went to live abroad and doesn't gamble at all now.

I've gone through all of the emotions with my kids, I've seen them begging on the streets for money – my own kids! I've thought at times that they don't belong to me, I still love them of course I do, I'll always love them but they are not kids really they're adults and I can't change how they live their lives.

I have one grandchild who is four years old, she has serious health problems, the worst kind of epilepsy it is possible to have and lots of other things wrong with her. She needs very special care that I can't give to her. Her mother (Maureen) is a serious drug addict and gave the baby to social services on the understanding that she would stay with foster parents only until Maureen got clean. Nobody helped Maureen to get clean, she wasn't given any support or anything and if anything she went further down hill and got more involved in drugs. There are no places in rehab centres because there are so many drug addicts; this country is rife with it. Maureen's going through a very rough time of it, knowing what's going on at the moment, the adoption hearings and everything She hasn't got any drugs inside, she's had to come off it in there, they give you some medication but basically they go cold turkey. I'm not stupid, I know that you can get to drugs still when you are in prison but we wouldn't smuggle them in there for her, no way and I make sure that she doesn't have any money sent in so that she has nothing to trade with. She's wanted to see her little girl while she's been inside but the social services keep fobbing her off, she cried and cried when I went to visit her, begging me to go to social services and force them to let her see the little one, she reckons that she must have some right to see her but I don't think she has any rights over the baby now. I told her 'What would be the point in them bringing the baby here anyway, you're only going to get in such a state if you see her.' Maureen begged the social services to help her to get into a rehab place but they did nothing.

I have only done that one visit to Maureen so far, my other daughter goes to see her, I got so upset in the visits room that I nearly walked out, we've had major rows, I broke down in front of her, you do everything, you say everything but it just goes on and on. Would you believe that she feels all at home there and she's really settled down with prison life. She was really hyper when I went to see her, she was so full of it I couldn't believe my ears, she's got her own room with a TV, there's a gymnasium and a swimming pool, the way she was going on you would think she was in flaming Butlins. I told my old next door neighbour about it, she's 92 years old and never heard anything like it in her life.

I'm very upset about my granddaughter going to strangers, if she hadn't had all of those problems I would have taken her, there's no doubt about that. I'm sixty now and I've seen her when she has her worst fits and such like and I know I couldn't cope. Also, I'm bringing up my grandson, he's eleven now and I've had him since he was five.

My son Mike lost his two kids through drugs. He was an addict and their mother still is, he got himself cleaned up and went abroad to live with his Dad. Mike works and saves and sends his money over for his kids, he works hard now and has really turned the corner., Mike and his ex were both on drugs. She (Mike's ex) went on the missing list altogether and then Maureen 'phoned us from Holloway and told us that she was in there.

One of my other daughters (Nicky) is an addict too. It's Nicky's son Jo who lives with me, I have a residency order to say that he stays with me, he's lived here since he was five and he's eleven now. Nicky got clean for a year and had another baby but she's back on it now and the baby is only a year old. I thought that she would be OK after being clean for a year, she was looking really sorted out. There's a possibility of me looking after the baby now. We can't live together, well, addicts can't live normal lives, things flare up and she can't handle it so off she goes. The baby lives with her at present, it hurts not to have the baby here.

In some ways it's easier when there's just me and Jo, when Nicky's here she gives Jo permission to do all kinds of things that I won't allow, he thinks then that he can do what she says because she's his mummy, I have to tell him that it's me

"My son Mike lost his two kids through drugs. He was an addict and their mother still is, he got himself cleaned up and went abroad to live with his Dad."

"There's a lot of pressure on me from my family to finish with him, I don't know with the baby and stuff, I felt sick all the way up here on the train, I'm sick of this – I don't want this for my life"

who has to make the decisions about what happens because I have the care of him. Jo was on the at risk register before he lived with me but as soon as I brought him here the social services didn't want to know anymore and just left me to get on with it. Jo always says that he would like us to get a big house and all live together and look after each other, he sees the world through rose coloured glasses, I couldn't live with them all, I couldn't cope. I tell Jo that this is how it's got to be, he sees Mummy when he sees her. He's cried, I've cried and we've both cried together. I don't get a look in when his mother is around; he always took more notice of her than he took of me when she lived here. It breaks his heart each time she moves out, he just wants to have us live together."

Maria is 60 years old; she has five children and several grandchildren. Three of Maria's children are heroin addicts, she has a daughter who is in prison, an eleven year old grandson who resides with her, a four year old granddaughter who is currently with foster parents and about to be adopted and a one year old grandson who lives with his mother currently but is on the 'at risk' register and may possible go to live with Maria.

Grandparents – attitudes or criticism from another generation

"My Dad wasn't very supportive at first, he tends to see everything in black and white, right and wrong, that was a struggle at first but he has come round a bit now. Young people today have a completely different lifestyle with so many added pressures than we had, you can see why they mess things up from time to time." *Alison 41, whose son is in prison.*

"My Mum thinks that I should disown him which is tough - when he got sentenced it really affected the relationship between myself and my Mum which was hard as I had no one to talk to about it all, I didn't want to talk openly about it to just anyone. His brother has told most people." *Angie 27.*

"My mother wanted the whole thing kept very quiet, she's very elderly and housebound now, she gave me cards to post to him, she didn't want her friends to see the address on the envelope." *Lorna 54, son 28.*

Families changing and splitting up

"My Mam and Dad are getting divorced, so that's something else to think about. It must be difficult for me Mam to cope. I don't want to know my Dad. He's found someone else. I think you always feel for your Mam more. I don't know why but that's how it is for me."

M.25, HMP Loudham Grange sentence 8 years served four. His daughter is aged 4.

"I have two girls aged 14 and 16 years old. I had been married for 21 years. She was the only proper girlfriend I ever had really, but she divorced me in June. The papers were served to me in prison. I haven't seen her since I was arrested and she doesn't like the girls to visit. I've only seen the girls four times in the two years but I 'phone them every other day. Everything is such a mess. I feel so bad about it all. Obviously our marriage wasn't right but I had planned to come back to England and we were going to get sorted. But I was arrested as soon as I got back in the country. We never really had time to talk about things. I thought we could work things out. I feel betrayed by her, how things were done, but what could I do about it? The worst part is the effect it's had on my daughters; not only is Dad in prison again, but now their parents are divorced. The girls are not happy about the divorce but they have no say. All the innocence has gone from my youngest girl because of prison and the divorce. She has seemed to be affected more. Her behaviour became odd and she is being seen by a psychologist at school to help her. My oldest girl seems to have become harder. It's her way of dealing with it all. But she's doing well at the college. You don't realize the effect you have on your kids." *R.42, sentence 9 years served 3. Loudham Grange two daughters aged 14 and 16.*

"My father was my best mate. He died when I was in prison last time and I still carry the guilt with me now. I should have been there when he was ill."

R.42 sentence 9 years served 3. Loudham Grange two daughters aged 14 and 16.

Death in the family

"You can't plan anything, you never know if he's going to be in or out. My Mom died when he was in there and he didn't come to the funeral, she didn't want him there in handcuffs. He'd been very close to her, he had a bedroom at her place and one at mine. How he got through her death I don't know. He was almost emotionless. I could have stayed home and cried and gone to the dogs but I had to visit him. I had to shower and dress and go there. He talked to me and he could do it." *Jeannie, her son 21 is in prison.*

"At the same time as the court cases, my Mum died, I didn't even cry about that until a year later, I had to put my grief into a box 'cos I just couldn't cope with everything at once and I had to be strong for my son." *Alison 41, son in prison.*

"We do tell Patrick about problems at home but if anything was wrong with us or his siblings we wouldn't, ill health and that, although, we did tell him when his Aunt got very ill with cancer, he used to ask after her all the time and a week or so before she died we told him that she didn't have long left to go and we got the prison to tell him when she went, he said that he was glad he had known all along but we wouldn't tell him if his Dad got very sick for example, he's very close to his Dad, we couldn't say if there was a problem with his Dad's health." *Louise, mother of Patrick, 24.*

emotions

NOTICE

Please be <u>very</u> careful when you enter this cell, budgie loose.

Take special care when you open and close the door to prevent injury to the bird.

Thank You.

CHAPTER FIVE - EMOTIONS

The swirling, often contradictory emotions felt by everyone caught up in these situations are often more painful to bear than any physical pain. Anger, shame, loss and isolation chart the course for these contributors.

Jealousy sleeplessness and guilt

"I'm not sure how things could be made easier for me, I don't really think they can be, maybe make sure you distance yourself at the trial!! Try and hate them!!! It was easier when we weren't together as we were good friends. I hope I can last the distance - I sometimes think he guilt trips me into staying with him - but you get over your differences - we get on so well. He does often get paranoid about how I feel about him. I think you should prepare yourself for the worst before they get sentenced, try and imagine what it's going to be like.... Sleep in single beds!! Nothing can really prepare you for that day when you come home alone. I still don't sleep properly but I don't take any tablets for that now." *Angie 27.*

"Sometimes we argue on the phone. I know he doesn't like it when I go out – but I would go completely mad if I didn't. I think the older blokes wind each other up, saying things like: 'What's your wife up to? Do you think she'll be there when you get out?' He is a jealous type, so it doesn't help when others say things and he starts thinking." *JW. Durham.*

"When I visit, I have to think what to wear. I once went in with a sleeveless top on and he said the blokes said I was too smart for him and I would find someone else." *Shirley, 25.*

Aware of how your partner feels?

"Now it is my partner's responsibility to bear my mistake too, but it is my action that has put my partner under incredible strain. I get so worried for my partner sometimes, my thoughts could be described as selfish, truth be known. I know no other way to sum or guess as to how my partner is coping without me. How will she pay the bills on time? How will the children cope without Dad? What if something were to befall any one of the children? Neighbours' children will learn of my imprisonment and tease my children. Neighbours will ignore and reject my partner's friendship. I now know my partner has always coped, that it was my lack of faith in her ability that has blinded me. To worry about your children whilst in prison breaks your heart and can bring about very serious depression. I now need, more than ever, the strength and skill to teach my children to take heed and learn that I do not want them to pass through these gates of pain."
Anon. written contribution from HMP Wolds.

"I don't go out that much because I'd feel guilty and he'd be telling me off for going out, things are not so clever."

"I have one little girl aged two and a half years. We sort of planned the pregnancy, not a definite time set, but we both knew we wanted kids. We were happy when we found out she was pregnant. We have good support from our families, which makes it easier. I have done the parenting course and I believe it should be available on the outside. Men might take their role as a father more seriously and with more responsibility if they really knew what it was about. I mean we should understand the woman's role more. I feel I do now and that's why our relationship is better and stronger. They visit me every week and have always done that. My daughter was about one and a half years old when I came in. She was too young to know and too young to tell her. But I must tell her when she's older. How I explain why I wasn't there….I think when children get older they might blame themselves for the mess. They need support and love from the parent that has been away. It's awful for my girlfriend having to cope and make all the decisions herself, but we do talk about issues now and discuss things together. The main problems are money, and the loneliness they feel. I'm very proud of my daughter and my girlfriend for dealing with all of this."
S. 24, HMP Wolds.

LOSS…AND FEELING WORTHLESS AS A PARENT

A father's view

"She brought him to see me when he was one week old. I thought it was awful to bring a baby into prison. It just didn't seem right, he was so new and clean. I didn't have a Dad when I was young. I'm never gonna see him do things for the first time. I want to be a Dad, a proper Dad. I feel other people have the father figure role with him and I do feel jealous of them. I think I'm just a name to him – it just happens to be Dad – not Fred. But deep down I think there is a bond between us." *Serving a 12 year sentence in HMP Wolds. age 27.*

A mother's view:

"I think about what it will be like to see them or touch them, but it hurts too much. I have to stop thinking about it. Some of the women here are helpful; I enjoyed doing the Family Matters course - I wish I was normal like them but I'm not. I'm trying not to do drugs but I don't know about the out. I've been in Phoenix House but it didn't help me. My younger kids are in care or fostered. I don't know who has them. I only have contact through Social Services and they're not much cop. Their Dad has no say in anything. It's all a mess but I do think about them sometimes. I hate it that I don't know who they live with or what the people are like. I never get to know anything - I suppose I'm not a fit mother because of the drugs. I wanted to be a good mother but the drugs came first." *C. 41, Low Newton.*

"She brought him to see me when he was one week old. I thought it was awful to bring a baby into prison. It just didn't seem right, he was so new and clean. I didn't have a Dad when I was young. I'm never gonna see him do things for the first time. I want to be a Dad, a proper Dad."

Serving a 12 year sentence in HMP Wolds. age 27

A daughter's view:

"My Mum has got bail; I'm waiting to meet her because I want her to come home with me. She still has to go back to court though so I don't know if it's a good thing that she's being let out this morning, I might just get used to her being around again and us being together then she'll probably have to go back to prison. They might give her probation or something but I don't think so because she's done too much wrong in the past. I live day to day as far as my Mum's concerned – that's the only way to take her"

Shona is 17 years old and was waiting at a visitors centre for her mother to be released from prison.

We all miss out.

"The children are everything. It's an old saying you don't realize how much you got until you haven't got it anymore. Coming into prison made me realize that I always miss them and feel sad all the time about what they've missed – what I've put them through and how much I miss out."

D. 28, HMP Holme House sentence 4 years.

When does the loss hit? *Young fathers talking to Martin Glynn, Swinfen Hall.*

"Obviously you go to court. You hear the sentence. That first night you was locked up...where did children come into your thoughts? At the point of sentencing or did you not think about that till later?"

"I was a failure and how could she ever respect me? I love my daughter, she is my life. I wish I'd been a better mother, a better person, but I can't change the past."

M. 43, Low Newton.

"Basically all that morning from the time I got up, I thought about my kids. Even when I got sentenced...that's all I could think about."

"Probably it was when I was sitting in the dock and the judge started to read the sentence and she just came into my mind, that I knew I wouldn't be there for her...I wouldn't be out to bring her up and look after her the way I should do."

"I got bail and I spent as much time as I could with the children - all that time. Then, when I was in the court and they said it - it was just shutting down something. I used to think, I've let them down. I'm trying to amend it you know."

Among prison parents the sense of loss is intense. But it is very different for men and women. It is different for the children of male or female prisoners too: Women on the outside strive hard to keep families intact when their son or partner is inside, even using almost a week's income and a whole day to get to the visit. "He must see his Dad," they'll frequently say. Because women are more likely to take children to visit, two thirds of fathers get to see their children. But for mothers in prison, fewer men visit with children or keep in touch. Less than half the mothers got visits from their kids. But one in five prison mothers said, "I don't want my child to see me here" and 42% said "My child wants to visit me but cannot." A key loss for men is not being there for the birth.

Not there when the baby is born

"I have one daughter who is eight years old now. She was very much a planned baby. My wife and I both wanted children. She was actually in labour when she came to visit me. She had the baby the next day. She was gutted that I wasn't there for the birth. The screws were great, they let me 'phone the hospital to find out what was happening. I actually spoke to my wife after she gave birth. That's the nearest I could get to being there, but it still couldn't replace me being present. She brought the baby in as soon as she could. When I got out last time, my little girl was seventeen months old. We didn't have any problems, she knew who I was. She had seen me every week. I saw her first steps when I was in the other prison. Each week there was something different to see or hear. My family live over on the west coast but they still come every week unless my daughter has something arranged. She has lots of activities going on in school time. I want her to have a normal life as much as possible. Why should she suffer because I'm in here?" *W. 44, HMP Wolds sentence 10 years served 2 years 6 months, he has one daughter of 8 years old.*

"I was in prison when my daughter was born. It was brilliant but shit at the same time." Interviewer: Why risk being away from her again? The second time I was put in prison I didn't really do anything. I was with some blokes who were doing cars up and the police said they were stolen, and because I'd been inside before, they thought I was involved. Her mother and I split up before I came into prison. I only found out she was pregnant just before I got sentenced so she was born when I was in here – that makes me feel crap about myself and for her. She was 28 days old when I first saw her, I didn't see her again until she was one year old. I have a good relationship with her mother, she still lets me see her. My Mam and sister bring her on visits. I had a good childhood. I was spoilt really. My Mam had a cot death before me, so I was fussed over. I wanted to be there for the birth. It was an accident, getting pregnant. We were both young and not right for each other, but that doesn't mean I can't be involved with my child. I don't have any rights as an unmarried father and that worries me. My ex has another child to someone she lives with and my little girl calls him 'Dad'. I get known as Daddy Mike and that really hurts me." *M.25, HMP Loudham Grange his sentence is 8 years, he has served four. Daughter aged 4.*

"I felt crap when I was in hospital having the baby, 'cos everyone asks about the Dad. What can you say or do? My family were there for me. When you are on your own you feel stupid. Everyone looks at you – and I am not stupid." *S. She is 18 years old now, the baby is 7 months. Partner is in HMP Durham.*

"My daughter is 13 months. By the end of the visit she's just starting to like be comfortable around me and she's climbing all over me and smiling at me. And that's it the visit is done and then two weeks or a month later she doesn't know me. I'm a pure stranger. She hasn't a clue who I am. I could be a prison officer."

"I can't talk to anyone, I work full time but I haven't told the people I work alongside. I don't know what will happen to our relationship while he's still in there, far less what will happen when he gets out, I don't know if we'll last that long."

Jo, 53.

"I was five months pregnant when he went away and I had to go through it all on my own, the labour and everything with just my seven year old little boy. I feel it's not happening to me, you know, like it's all happening to someone else." *Linny.*

Staying indoors - isolation

"It's been a nightmare, everything they go through, you go through, I expect all of the women say the same thing. The age difference doesn't matter to us; it might to other people but not to us. I don't go out because I'd feel too guilty if I was enjoying myself, Bob tells me to go out and have a good time but I can't, I'd feel too guilty with him in there, so when I'm not at work I stay home. I'm a nurse and a lot of people I work with don't know where Bob is – I'm not ashamed of him though. I say that he's in rehab or away, they can accept that he's in rehab because they know that he had a drugs problem but rehab's different to jail, it's not so shameful and a lot of nurses are straight laced." *Dee, 47.*

"When it first happened I was good for nothing - I wouldn't leave the house, I was drugged up to my eyeballs, I couldn't see my way through. It sounds harsh but I think if he'd have died it would be easier, as now I feel a similar grief but instead I know he's out there and I can't see him. I want to try and stay with him for the whole time but it does seem like it's going to be difficult, I have to try and make it work. I keep worrying about whether I'll be able to handle it for that amount of time. I think the hardest thing is him not being here, I can't talk to him when the kids go to bed, and the nights are really lonely for me. Friends don't always want to hear it all as they have their own life. Partners you can have a moan to, or talk to them about anything, the small things. I have written him letters before but I can't find the words to say to him at the moment - I just feel too distraught." *Angie 27.*

"One of the worst things about it all was the isolation. We had moved to this house fairly recently before my husband went to prison, so my friends and family didn't live locally. At one stage my Mum came to stay but that made it harder for me to cope with." *Elise, 35.*

"I don't go out but that's not because of babysitting, it's down to money." *Lena.*

"I don't know I have my good days and my bad days. Yesterday I was in tears but today I am alright. I go into an empty flat every day which is the hardest part. I'm actually at home now by myself. It's coming up to Christmas now and both our birthdays, it's a time you're meant to be with your family." *Jane, 25.*

Margaret 74, There's something wrong with my son.

Margaret's story shows how parenting is a lifelong endeavour. Her son's story illustrates how confused the services are in dealing with his multiple problems.

"He went into prison 3 times just last year and there's been other times. The first time he went in I was shocked. I was half expecting it but on the other hand I was hoping that he wouldn't go in. It was shock, devastation really. I knew that they might have sent him down at the time; the solicitor warned me that he might get a sentence. He has been caught by the police enough times, but it is an awful shock. I didn't go to court that time he got sent down but I have been to court to give evidence... but it didn't help him. I think that I've been twice when he's asked me but he didn't ask me the last time. The solicitor rang up and said I'm ever so sorry but they have sent him to prison. I said well maybe there's one consolation that perhaps it will dry him out but of course it didn't. He comes out and he did just the same.

I think he got 12 months and did 6 the first time and several times he's got 6 months and done three and he's misbehaved in between and got time added on. You see if he's already been in there a month on remand and then they sentence him to two months he's out in a month which is ridiculous in my opinion. I said why don't they put him on community work but they won't do because of his drink, well I suppose that is the snag. I just don't understand how he's got in such a state, I really can't.

This has been going on a long time. The G.P said he was going to cure him in 1980. In '82 he became ill and went into a mental hospital, he went in again in '84 'cos the G.P took the tablets of him 'cos he said that he didn't need them. Then he stopped taking the tablets of his own free will and according to the law nobody can make him take them, they can't section him because he hasn't done anything wrong enough. So in other words if he attacked an old woman or a child they could section him, which doesn't make sense to me.

It will be 6 years this July since he left this house. Before that he was gradually getting worse with his drink. At first he'd go to sleep and wake and cry for me, fair enough he wanted a bit of company and he'd had a drop too much, things weren't too bad then, he slept it off. Then it got worse and instead of sitting down and going to sleep he was going outside in the street and shouting at the people passing by, which got him into trouble. Then one night he stood over me and threatened to kill me. I spoke to the psychiatrist about it and he said that if it happens again then I should call the police, which I did. They said if I got the police then they could do something and I thought they meant they would put

"It was an awful thing having to call the police on my son."

> "I couldn't sleep - I was given antidepressants - these made me so off my face I didn't even know what day it was. I have tried thinking about the things that are good; that I should be thankful that he is alive there is someone that is always worse off than yourself."
>
> *Alison 41. Her son was in prison.*

him in a mental hospital but they took him and put him in his own home but he just can't cope, he needs supervision and help. It was an awful thing having to call the police on my son. I think what would have happened that night if I'd put up with his drunkenness would he have got better, but I don't think he would have and I got to the stage where I just couldn't take anymore. All the neighbours are nice and they come in the shop and say that there is something wrong with him. I shall be very sad if my son does go back into prison 'cos I feel that there's somebody not doing what they should do or could do. He comes out exactly the same every time he goes away, goes straight for the bottle of cider. It's not doing him any good to keep going in and out of prison. He isn't getting the right kind of help."

Depression and medication

"I used to be strong and now I'm just a dithering wreck. When he was sentenced (re-arrested at the gate when she expected release) it took my life away from me. I was put onto medication… I came to breaking point… but time is a great healer. Until he's out - nothing is going to change, I've had to try and pull myself together. I think without my kids I would have topped myself by now. I have two children who were nine and six at the time - they thought he was going to come home. In a way it's not such an issue for them as he isn't their father and he was already in prison when we met so they cope with him still being away. It's so difficult to explain what it's like when it happens - it completely blew my head trying to comprehend another 10 years away from him just when I thought it was all over. Last Christmas was the worst I've ever had, I just didn't want to know, as it was so hard – yeah, that definitely was a really bad time for all of us. After he was put away again I couldn't stop crying for 2 months - I went off sick from work - it wasn't good for the kids to see. The thing is I've made my choices in life, I've chosen to stay with him and now I just have to try and live with it. When he had his transfer it was so far away it made everything ten times worse, I've now had to go back onto medication. The furthest I had been before was 20 minutes in the motorway. Travelling isn't really me and makes me really stressed."
Angie 27, two children, partner inside.

"I told a few of my friends and they were very supportive and it was splashed across the front of the paper and that was the worst, big headline and photo and I felt that everyone was looking at me as I walked down the street, in the end we felt that paranoid. In the 8 weeks my daughter was off she had a mental break down and overdosed, she took off in her car one night and I couldn't find her, got her on her mobile told her that I have to call the police which brought her to her senses and she came home. She had to have mental health involved. She felt in a way that her brother had been taken away from her, that there was no control and she couldn't see him, couldn't do anything with him, she took it harder than I did. I think it was because I was more concerned for her that I could handle that bit better." *Lorraine 45.*

"I have a husband and four kids. M. is the eldest, it is four years since he was released from prison and I wish I could have talked about my feelings then the way I can now. I have lain on the bathroom floor, curled up in a ball trying to stop the scream coming out of me, not wanting the rest of the family to hear me crying. It's hard for parents. The men deal with it differently. Me and my husband were at loggerheads, he couldn't see how it was all affecting me and that made things worse. My daughter was very upset and one day we all just started screaming at each other about how we all felt, things changed then, we started working together as a family instead of against each other."
Mother of ex heroin addict.

"Mum wouldn't go out the house because of the dirty looks and her drinking, she shut herself off, she was drinking because of him. When he says we are in the wrong we think, you did all this, you did worse. He hates being wrong. She just sat and stared at the wall. I wasn't around to see it all I didn't stick around; I went to live with my boyfriend. I came round now and again but everyone was always upset and I couldn't handle it." *K. 16.*

"I've always smoked but I smoke more now, I'm on anti depressants now, I told my doctor everything, she's really nice, I can talk to her and she says she understands, I don't think she does understand but she's nice."
Dee 47, mother of two. Her partner received a five year sentence.

Shame – press and neighbours

"Seeing it in the paper didn't help: 'man in jail for his wife's' four year affair'. Mum used to get loads of grief from other people, with filthy comments, but then they apologised to her when they knew more about the truth. I was sick of hearing 'oh your Mam cheated on your Dad, so I told them all the truth'. Once they realised what he'd done wrong they started to talk to her again. Even my Dad's brother who we thought hated her has started beeping and waving as he drives past. Everybody knows everybody else's business round here" *K 16.*

"The story did come out in the paper but it wasn't too bad. If anyone did actually say anything I think I'd flip. The whole thing has totally overwhelmed me. Now I look back I think the time has gone reasonably quickly but then I still have another 8 years of this left to go." *Angie 27.*

" I told a few friends and they were very supportive and it was splashed across the front page of the newspaper and that was the worst - big headline and photo and I felt that everyone was looking at me as I walked down the street, in the end, we felt that paranoid."

Anon mother of son sentenced to 2 years.

"The local paper reported everything and I was devastated, friends at work were wonderful, they said – today's news is no more than tomorrow's fish and chip paper, most people have been very decent."

Lorna 54.

"The story hit the front page of the newspaper and the kids got loads of grief at school - it was sheer hell." *Elaine 35, her husband received a prison sentence.*

'Phone calls were welcome but they always made you feel flat inside afterwards. We just got through one day at a time. I was terrified and still am in case anyone finds out. I only told my sister. Everyone else thought she was not well and I was looking after the little one until she felt better. I don't know what I would have done if anyone in the village had found out. Fortunately my daughter lives far away." *S. daughter sentenced to six months.*

"The newspapers wrote lots about it and got it all wrong, but there wasn't particularly any backlash apart from some gossip locally."
Stuart 32, his wife is in prison – he takes care of their three children.

"The whole thing was in the papers, it made the front page. I didn't want it to be there. I don't know whether it was the way they put it or the way I perceived it but I felt to blame for what my brother had done. It felt like it was us that got all the flack. I didn't expect it to come out in the media as much as it did. I remember there was photo and it was in the headlines, we were passing the newsagent and his story headline was on the board outside. I was so shocked, when we went in to buy the paper I thought that the guy behind the counter knew we were buying the paper just because my brother was in it. My reaction was that I lied to everyone about it and told them he didn't do it, that he was innocent. I think that I lied for all of our sake 'cos I was so ashamed and embarrassed." *Kerrie 24, her brother was given a prison sentence.*

"There was shame cos we'd never experienced prison, the unknown, you've got the shame the devastation, you lose your son, as soon as he's sentenced, he's taken away, the whole control's gone, that's your son taken away from you, you can't do anything about it, you can't see them, you don't know where they've gone, although he's 18, he's still your son. I found it hard 'cos there was things I wanted to say to my son such as can you see what 's happened now, but I also wanted to see if he's OK. When he went to prison the first night we didn't hear anything, you imagine everything what's going on in prison, so many stories and TV programmes, the first 48 hours is awful. You get very angry, angry at society, with the system and at yourself that it's your son that's gone. You think 'what did I do wrong, why has this happened to me?" *Lorraine 45, whose son was sentenced to two and a half years.*

Neighbours

"I just feel life is an uphill struggle. We can't plan like other people. It's hard to think of the future. I've had to move house. We were having trouble with the neighbours. They called us names and the bloke's brother in law worked at the prison so I just did not trust them. Anyway we moved. It was the best thing to do but it was expensive. But I felt I had to protect the kids. We get no bother where we are and the kids like it. The only thing is the youngest is getting picked on at school not because of his Dad but because he is the new kid. The teachers are trying to sort it out. So that's another hurdle to jump. He has been punished and all our lives have been changed because of it." *C. her husband is in Acklington.*

"He could have been out on HDC but we blocked that, we definitely can't have him here you see, his friend from across our street died while they were using together and his family are blaming us. Before Will was sent to prison he was on the bus coming home one day and people from where we live were shouting 'murderer' on the bus at Will." *Mary 48, visiting her son who is 22.*

"We live on a small council estate and everybody knows everybody's business and because of this we've had threatening letters and 'phone calls and even been shouted at in the street, its horrible let me tell you but Bob and me, we can take it better, better than the kids I mean, it's worse for them having to suffer things." *Geraldine, grandmother of Adam and Sarah.*

"The next door neighbour started giving us abuse for various things - he made lots of complaints, it got to a point where I didn't want to go home as I was too scared, he created havoc for my family, it was a day to day hell, a horrendous experience. At the beginning I was so angry at him for the things he was doing, in a way I felt sorry or pity for him that he felt the need to do those things, now I just hate him. My neighbour even followed my daughter at one point, he was a teacher as well which made my daughter lose all faith in school and she didn't want to go. I feel that I am very angry about a lot of what has happened, the trauma we have gone through, the trauma the neighbour has put us through, it just feels so unjust, but you'd go mad about it if you thought about it too much. We nearly moved house because of the neighbour but we decided that why should he drive us out of our own home? We just want to get on with our lives." *Elise 35.*

"At first I didn't dare go out, I was always on my guard, thinking that people were pointing the finger but it was OK, even my neighbours have been good with me." *Jackie 37, mother of three children, her husband is in prison.*

"He was turned out from his house because of his behaviour. He is schizophrenic and paranoid. He would leave at night and stand on the street shouting 'I know you're out there, I'll get you, you can't hide from me'."

"It nearly killed me all of this, I'm an honest kind of person and I brought them up alright, one son going to jail was bad enough but two of them.... The shock, I lost over a stone in weight in the space of a week and I couldn't stop crying, I thought I was going to die. The shame of it, that's taken me more than anything."

Sandra, visiting her son Robbie 25.

"The story hasn't come out in the media yet. I'm really worried about it coming out, if it does I think I'll go away for the weekend, I'm dreading it. My daughter was very close to her brother. She's told a couple of her closest friends but one of them is making her feel really uncomfortable about it."
Jill 47, her teenage son is serving a sentence.

Shame – unable to live your life – the impact on a parent.

"When he first went to prison I didn't go out, didn't want to leave the house as I thought everyone was looking at me. I blamed myself, kept asking myself questions such as - 'why didn't I do more to help him, had I been in denial before and just couldn't face up to the reality'? I have been very lucky to have a friend who has listened to everything. I have found that running a business has helped as it has made me keep going. I couldn't sleep - I was given antidepressants - these made me so off my face I didn't even know what day it was. I have tried thinking about the things that are good; that I should be thankful that he is alive there is someone that is always worse off than yourself.

It's very hard to explain to someone who hasn't been through it - I just don't think I could go through it again - it just hurt so much. The story went round like wildfire - lots of distorted gossip - most of my closest friends were good, however some don't even speak to me anymore. I have had lots of support.

There was no media publicity, which I'm very grateful for, as I don't think I could have coped with that. My other son didn't let anyone know at work - I think that was just his way of coping with it. I didn't like going to Glen Parva - everyone there made me feel so guilty like I was the one who had committed the crime. I think the hardest thing has been trying to accept that my son would do that and that it isn't my fault, that was tough to try and stop blaming myself. But you can't go back, you can only go forward. SHARP really helped through that to come to this point. I think more information is needed." *Alison 41.*

"The worst part for me were the prison searches, not so much for me as worrying for my Mum, she's an old lady and I felt demeaned on her behalf, that humiliation was the worst thing. I felt like I'd done something wrong, we were treated as suspects, they, (prison officers) took a blanket approach towards visitors and I always felt very uncomfortable. We were presumed guilty until proven innocent."
Claire, mother of a 22 year old sentenced on drug charges.

"When he was first arrested I didn't tell anyone either, and I had to keep taking time off to attend the police station. But I met this woman whose son was charged with manslaughter and her husband is a JP. So you see there are so many in the same boat." *Jeannie, whose son now twenty one, has been in repeated trouble since he was fourteen.*

Anger

"I was really angry at first when he got sent down, but I've got used to it. What else can you do? You've got to go on. I wasn't very nice to him when he went in. I used to say things like 'you'll never see this baby.' I don't now why. I suppose I was just angry, I wanted him at home. I hate him being in there. I know I wind him up. We argue on the 'phone. Sometimes it makes me feel better then other times I think what can he do? I hate it when he says he shouldn't be in prison. He did wrong and he is being punished. He says he'll change and I think he'll change. He said he would for the baby."
S. She is 18 years old now, the baby is 7 months. Partner is in HMP Durham.

"My ex boyfriend was sent down for two years. We have just split up while he is in prison. I found out from the staff that he has been sending all his VO's to another girl. How crap do I feel? How stupid am I? I did visit when he sent me the VO. I sent him money. I'm just glad that my kids are not his and he has no say over them or any rights to them. I've done loads for him, practically and emotionally. I didn't know he was an addict but apparently this other girl takes drugs in for him. I don't use drugs and I won't be used by him. I am just so mad at myself for standing by him and making a fool of myself. I've wasted time on him and sometimes putting him first. When someone is in prison you think how bad it is for them - you stop thinking about your own needs. I think I am still in shock about it all. When I think about going to visit and queuing with all the scumbags, I could scream. I've spent loads of money on him sending postal orders making sure he has clothes etc. And all the time he was even cheating on me whilst inside! Some people are just nasty. When I think back how I tried to talk to him about me or the kids it has always been about what he has to do without or it's someone else's fault – when sometimes I think he should consider others. I know it can't be much fun but then some days are not a bundle of laughs for me. I don't miss going to the nick or waiting for the post anymore."
C. visiting Holme House.

"When I think about the course it is better than nothing. But I do keep asking why should I have to do it, but the social workers keep reminding me that I want to help him so I keep on with it. The prison is out of the way but all kinds of people come there. It is amazing the number who have committed these offences. I get mad about the different sentences people get around the country, nothing is the same. It's hard to know what to think about sometimes when I visit. He does not tell me too much about the course but I know they talk to each other inside. That's their support. They talk about their crimes and I get the chance to talk to the social worker and probation staff.

I hate it when he says he shouldn't be in prison. He did wrong and he is being punished. He says he'll change and I think he'll change. He said he would for the baby."

"You just don't envisage in your wildest dreams that this could happen to you. I felt like I was on another planet. I didn't even know what day it was."

I don't feel like a woman any more. There is so much to think about: the house, the kids, my husband. And I am in and out of hospital. I had an operation on my back and I need physio three times a week. I'm busy with the solicitors at present sorting out his pension and tax. I'm involved with the services. I'm making sure everything is alright for his coming home. There is always something to see to. One day when he rang I was in the middle of making Sunday dinner. The lads were arguing and he told me he was on association going to play table tennis. I could just say I wish the fuck I had time to play table tennis and put the 'phone down. I have to be strong so much of the time."*C. her husband has a seven year sentence, she has two teenage sons and is on anti depressants.*

"I was so angry with Mark because he was so selfish and didn't give any thought to what he was doing to my Mum, Dad, sisters and me. He never did think about what he should have been to me as my brother. It's very different, what you expect from a brother to what you have with your sisters, a different relationship. He's so tall and handsome our Mark, I should have been able to have nights out with him and show him off to my friends, be able to be proud at having such a gorgeous brother, instead he was a 'smack head' how could I be proud of that? I couldn't tell my Mum about my feelings around our Mark for a long time because I felt that she had enough problems, when I did tell Mum, she told me that I had to tell our Mark how I felt, how angry with and hurt by him I was, so I did tell him and he apologised, I think he really meant it too." *Christie, the prisoner's sister.*

"You get very angry, angry at society, with the system and at yourself that it's your son that's gone. You think; what did I do wrong? Why has this happened to me?" *Lorna 54, her son was involved with drugs.*

Denial: everything's OK, or is it?

"When I see him or speak to him I don't tell him the truth, I try to be strong to him. I just don't think he realises just how difficult it is for us on the outside. I am trying to look at both sides and the difficulties we face. How do you get through the day? You get through the day because you have to. The kids help me a lot, they keep me laughing - I really don't want to cry in front of them." *Angie 27.*

"We didn't say how bad we were feeling and I am sure she didn't tell us how bad it was inside. 'Phone calls were kept short. I don't think anyone could have handled long detailed conversations. It was our way of coping but it still haunts me and I am sure it will forever." *S. daughter served six months.*

"You learn what to say and what not to say to them, you start not putting things in letters that they could take the wrong way, you read them two or three times before you send them. We are very honest and talk about everything, if you haven't got that communication you are lost because the system sets out to destroy you and everything you have together." *Lucy 34, coping with her five children while her partner is inside.*

"No, I don't tell him how I feel, I do love him and I want the baby but I don't think I can keep doing this, I think I'm going to tell him today that that's it, I'm not coming back, but I don't know because then he'll kick off in there and he'll feel bad and I'll feel bad, I don't know." *Dawn 22, is three months pregnant – she visits her boyfriend.*

"I told him most of my problems but I was careful, he was powerless and there's no point putting pressure on when he can't do anything about it." *Jane 38, her husband was remanded in custody, they have two daughters.*

"I used to keep most things to myself, he was locked up 24/7 and I didn't want to worry him." *Elaine 28, partner sentenced to six months, she has three children.*

"I've always still shared my problems with him, there haven't been any major things but you know, like when the kids are getting on my nerves and things. I write about those things in letters because when I visit that's our time and I don't want to have us thinking about problems because it's the only time we have together." *Jackie 37, coping with three children while her husband serves a 3 1/2 year sentence.*

"At the beginning there were lots of things that went on that I didn't tell him, I kept plodding on, then it all got in such a state and I burst out with everything. He said I should have been telling him and now I do, I tell him everything rather than my Mum and Dad to keep worrying them, I need his opinions, it makes it easier to cope, I talk it all through with him."
Jasmine 23, takes 22 month old baby to visit her father.

"Some people have been great since he came home, others not, he went into our local pub the other night and asked for a pint of bitter, he was told that he wasn't welcome there, that really hurt him, he was upset"

Lorna 54 supporting her son Owen 28.

Keeping up the 'Macho', another form of denial?

"Men don't like to admit to being scared, they think it's not manly, especially I think when they come from the north, they have to keep being macho. Tommy looks as hard as nails but he's not hard inside." *Lucy 34, partner serving 5 months.*

"I was hiding my financial problems from my family. I think it was out of some daft sense of pride, wanting to be 'the man' of the family. So I didn't tell anyone not even my wife. I would now. I turned away from my family. I used to think I had high standards in everything but I think it was really a kind of stubbornness. But d'you know I've met a lot of good people in prison. Some of them have been to the rock bottom like me, so there's no bullshit. I think now with hindsight I really could have found a way to have told my family what was going on and got their support." *This contribution is taken from: Kirklevington Grange Press 'You feel like a stranger', thanks to Chris, writer in residence.*

"We were both trying to be brave for each other but inside I was worried about everything. I didn't know how my family was going to survive." *Elise 35.*

Hiding the court appearance.

"Nobody knew I was going to court. I felt so ashamed and guilty about what I had done that I couldn't tell anyone. The only person who I could talk to was the probation officer and to some extent the solicitor and barrister. I never told my parents or my partner. The probation officer had to tell my partner and he had to tell my parents after I was sentenced." *L. 43, Low Newton.*

We share our worries.

"We had just moved to a new area and I didn't know anybody. At one point I thought I was going to move back again because I was so lonely. I had to tell him about my problems because I had nobody to talk to around here." *Laura 23, mother of two sons, her husband received a three month sentence.*

"I tell Shaun about all of my problems, I didn't at first but I do now, he tells me about his problems so now I tell him what mine are, it makes me feel better, it makes him feel better." *Christina 25, her partner is awaiting sentence, their three week old baby was born while he was in prison.*

"I tell him about my problems but he's a bloke and bloke's just don't understand, I've got family problems but I've got my Mam, we are really close." *Teresa 24, supporting her partner through a three year sentence.*

"Tommy looks as hard as nails but he's not hard inside."

young **offenders**

"The last time Lisa came out she was so drugged up she was like a walking zombie, I had to take her to the doctors, she was climbing the walls because she was so high, I couldn't get her down, it took us three months to sort her out. She had been asking for medication when she was inside and they kept dishing it out to her, they (prison staff) will give them drugs willingly because it keeps them quiet."

CHAPTER SIX - YOUNG OFFENDERS

How does it feel to be separated from your family and friends?
"I feel am upset, true to say. My co-defendant got bail the other day. Not upset yeah – but kind like angry. I feel I've coped well yeah, like I have been here 7 months. I watch TV, read a lot, I read my bible and I do my work. (Shows interviewer a folder of drawings). My Mum yeah, I 'phone her and my girl, yeah, I write her and 'phone her. My friends I don't really write to them, cause they understand what it's like in here. You know who your friends are when you get in here ya get me? I get like three visits a week from me Mum and me bredrins (on remand). When I get out I'm going to stay with my Mum but won't be so bonified (close) with my friends cause I don't really look at them the same, as my good friend snitched on me. So I kinda don't have it with him no more."
C. 15, Feltham YOI.

One by one, young offenders described a very disrupted family life, or other family members in trouble and frequent experience of being in care. J. 16, on remand in Feltham YOI, talks about his life:

"What makes me angry is my loved ones are outside and don't see me. My family is messed up. It is usually the Dad that turns away, but this time it was my Mum. My Mum's pregnant and when she visits she wants me to help her. I want her to give me the attention. My Mum would take money from my robberies, she knew how I got the money. I've got six sisters, three have been in care. I was in care for about two months, my Dad took me out and I went to live with him. I had gold in my hand when I went to live with my Dad. But I had a label – anything goes wrong – I got the blame and at school they knew my Dad beat me, and would threaten to tell him if I did any little thing wrong. My Dad humiliated me in front of my friends at school.

I've never been in prison before. My Dad has been in prison in Kingston Jamaica. When he came to England he was caught smuggling at the airport and went straight to prison for six months. What I see is, either I'm going to be lucky like my Dad who has never been in jail since – or unlucky like my brother. He went into a secure unit when he was 15 for 18 months, came out and went back into prison for 8 years. He's served 6 years and is looking to get parole."

J. has no trust left in any one yet he talks both about not needing anyone and at the same time longing for their support:
"When my brother went to jail I was told, but because he never wrote to me, I thought he was dead. I got used to living a street life in a gang. No money, I

liked it. I haven't thought about what to do when I get released – it's a bit too far ahead. I won't need support. I'm a soldier. I will set myself targets. My stepmum will look after me when I come out – pay for me to get out of prison. I'm waiting to speak to my brief. I will need support from my family. I never see my personal officer. I told the counsellor about myself and it got back to the prison officers – they started laughing about it and banging on my cell door and cussing about it. They went to the pub and had a pint on it."

But sometimes J. does long for a different future – one that includes both a personal relationship and some work and achievement:
"When I get out I'm going to get myself a beautiful girlfriend. I will call her my wife. At weekends I will work with my stepmum – definitely. During the week I will go to college and get my GCSE's." *He has been on remand 5 months.*

Where have they taken him?
"My son was 15 years and 3 months when he was sent down (motoring offences) and I didn't know where he was. I didn't know if he'd been taken to the local Young Offenders Centre or the secure unit. For two days I didn't know where he was. He was allowed to ring me two days later. I had rung around and I did speak to Glen Parva but they said he wasn't booked in. In fact he was there but he hadn't been booked in yet when I rang.

It was December 12th before Christmas. I didn't know anything about the system. I didn't know what I could or couldn't take to him. He looked so small, it's horrendous seeing that – the others looked about 20. You can't imagine the initial impact it has, the first time. But he wasn't beaten up because he knew the other lads in there from the estate and they sort of took him under their wing like." *Jeannie.*

Lorraine (40) visits her twenty-year-old daughter – Lisa, it is Lisa's second time in prison, and she is currently serving four months and served six months when she was seventeen.

"This time she's in for stealing and the last time it was for a violent offence, her co-accused got five years then so it goes to show that Lisa didn't play a very big part in it all. I have two other children who will probably come to visit her. I've travelled from Hertfordshire, if they had sent her anywhere else I would have been stumped because I don't have a car, if they ship her out to somewhere else I'll be stumped. There is a shortage of YOI's for girls, so it means further distances to travel for parents, also, young girls are put in with the older women until they are convicted and that can go either way. They can pick up bad habits

> "He wants flash cars and flash clothes and he wants it all now. His sister did well (she's older) and he was always hearing about his sister he had a lot to do to follow after her."
>
> *Jeannie.*

from the older women who are more used to being in bother or the women can look out for them, kind of mother them in a way. The last time Lisa came out she was so drugged up she was like a walking zombie, I had to take her to the doctors, she was climbing the walls because she was so high, I couldn't get her down, it took us three months to sort her out. She had been asking for medication when she was inside and they kept dishing it out to her, they (prison staff) will give them drugs willingly because it keeps them quiet. She was working for agencies but she will have to start again when she comes out, I doubt that the agencies will give her a job. I have a good boyfriend, he is very supportive, he will probably visit her and will definitely write to her because they get on well, I'm amazed he's still around. It was Lisa's choice to come to prison, she could have had community service but she had a couple of outstanding fines and stuff so she asked to be given time, no one could understand that she didn't want to stay out of prison."

Jeannie - I'm grateful he's not an addict but supply is just as addictive

"He'd been in trouble before for shoplifting and fighting. He'd been fined for possession of Cannabis. But this was his first time inside. I kept thinking what's he doing here? We believe he's got some form of autism. He's got no fear – never has had. But he was disruptive. He was expelled from school yet his SATS results at 14 were excellent in maths and science. The school tried to keep him as I liased so closely. When he was excluded he was hanging around on street corners drinking, smoking draw, shoplifting and fighting. At 15 he was in for 15 months in a YOI in Rugby. It was a zero tolerance regime which aggravated things. For example he ran over the grass and lost 7 days. Then when he was bullied inside he got in trouble fighting and lost a month. Now the YOI has separated the under 18's and the 18-21's but not then. He got no training until later on a STAR programme where he got some anger management and I saw on the out that he did learn a few things when he tried to calm me down once after a traffic incident when I was driving.

There was a really good youth club leader round here who had known my son since he was little, he was really good, but the funding's not there. Where we live there are students everywhere, The students got raided and bailed – one of them's a law student. We had a police raid and I got arrested too. Traces of

substance were found in the entry which I had nailed up and people had been coming over the wall. He's now on remand, I was released. There's times when I was on police bail - it was very hard for me to keep my mouth shut with him about the seriousness of this charge. His sister is always there for him.

She visits him but it is embarrassing for her. One day she saw two of her clients in the visiting room – hardly a fact to be proud of for her to say it's her brother. There is no need to say it 'cos I know how I felt and how he felt. It was Mothers Day when we were arrested. The police brought flowers when they came and said they had a warrant to search for a Class A drug. I felt I would die. I thought I were going to die. I felt ill. I understand how people mess thereselves. I'd not slept and I was eating for comfort. I couldn't plan. What will happen? What about work? The Mortgage? It was different completely. I can't live like that. These kids live differently they like it risky and exciting. But when a little time had passed I'd become a bit arrogant and thinking if they charge me this is what's going to happen. If they do... I shall tell them... you get all 'up' you see.

I do write to him but I don't write letters I just send cards. I can't waffle and I can't go into deep emotions. He knows I'm there when he gets the cards and I only have to put a short message on it. That's how I cope with writing. Also I don't think my emotions should be shared with a prison officer, so I don't say it. At Christmas I'd been so worried about him being in there, and yet 18 months after he came out he told us what a laugh they'd had in there at Christmas. Throwing stuff and shouting etc. He was my baby. It was Christmas, I was so worried…well they made the best of it in there, they had to. I can't risk it again if he comes home. I just hope he'll turn hisself around. He smokes Cannabis. I'd sooner him smoke C than drink alcohol. He's not cheeky to me or untidy in the house. He likes nice things. Now he's met someone inside who's in for computer fraud he wants to try that! He's got good conversation skills he can talk you round.

When I think back over everything I feel things happen for a reason. Maybe if he'd been on the outside he might have been involved in a murder? It was a Christmas Eve I would've done anything to have him home, my Mum had just died. But this happened - at least he was inside. (his best friend was involved in a murder, a shooting, drugs related. The friend is serving a life sentence and some of his family members have been sentenced for perverting course of justice.) When he's out you don't stop worrying. He'd be with me then off with his friends. If he'd got a flat, which he'd wanted, I'd have to store the furniture. I used to think I couldn't bear it if he didn't live at home. But now perhaps I'd feel relieved if he said he was going to live in another country. But then how would I manage to visit him? But if he got a girlfriend a bit like his sister, that might help. He is just stagnating it's a waste of a young life.

Round here, you see the 15 and 16 year olds on bikes act as runners. You see the flash trainers and you know they've got no jobs and their Mums have got no work. You don't need to be told. I can see. So if I know it everybody knows it. My son isn't manipulated – he's a manipulator in fact. It's like the lion's fallen out of the pack when he's not here. The others hang around doing nothing. When he's out he motivates them. They've got money. They go on holiday abroad. They buy flats – property. They know who the undercover police are - they taunt them! At first he was buying and selling cars.

I'm grateful he's not an addict but I think supplying is as addictive as the drug itself. That buzz with the money, the deals, three mobile phones. Yeah it's like Wall St. Some prison officers are kind and considerate to families some are human but there are some I'd spit on they're so nasty."

"When I ask him why he's not applied for benefit he says 'I'm not going to answer somebody's questions for £40,00 a week.' How many people live like that?"

"It was amazing... I can't... I was just stood there and watching – my baby come out and then when it come out and started crying ... it was the best feeling ever."

Young prison fathers – special issues they face

Young fathers ages 19-21 Swinfen Hall discuss fatherhood with Martin Glynn. Between them these 5 speakers have 11 children.

Father absence

Interviewer: "Interestingly enough, everybody here mentions my Mom'. In my case my father left. He abdicated that responsibility and then he died. Talk a little bit about our fathers – 'cos our fathers are a little bit to blame for the lack of information we have about parenting – sons in particular. Has anybody got any views on fathers' input into any of this?"

"Yeah, I think that's important really 'cos when I was young my father left my Mom for a short while before he died. And basically what I learned from him – 'cos I did know him for a short while before he died – but basically what I learned from him was I ain't gonna leave my kids. So that's it. I'm never gonna leave my kids."

"My Dad left us as well when I was about 7. I still see him you know but because he lives quite far away from where we live he didn't really have much contact with me or my child. But when he comes over I mean I love him to bits. He's learned me a lot I suppose when I was young. He's still there for us you know and if I every really need him he's always there at the end of the day."

"My father was really young also. He'd come back you know, to see me and my brothers and sisters. But you know we ain't his priority so he didn't put in 100% although he tried. He didn't do it right but he tried...so he got in a situation."

Are fathers different from other young offenders?

"They tar all of us with the same brush. Someone who is a father should be treated more like an adult. 'Cos we are with kids here. We're all treated as kids. I think, 'cos I'm a father I should be treated more like an adult and not treated like I'm some delinquent you know. I feel like I'm growing in myself and being treated like a childish person – I don't think it helps you grow in any way."

"I take responsibility for my kids even though I'm still in prison. I still have my say in what happens and what should happen in the future. My girlfriend's aware of that and I make as much effort as I can to keep in contact and I know what's going on out there."

There at the birth?

"I didn't actually cry or anything like that. It's like I was just waiting there watching my girlfriend in pain and that. It's like our baby came out, I cut the cord, I saw it was a boy and I run to the phone and called my my Mum. I said it's Timothy junior I knew his name."

"I just wanted to hold her it was like magic."

"I haven't had the chance to do anything but in my mind I just grow. I just wanna do something. I need to like earn to be called a father. I done nothing yet."

A father and an inmate: what's your role?

Did you plan on being a father at a young age?

"I was shocked at first then frightened. But I was brought up in a big family so I thought it ain't gonna make no difference. I thought it'd be alright. I'd still be me."

"When she said that…I don't know… I was a bit nervous – very nervous, then I was excited. But I was worried in the situation I was as well, like at the moment."

"I don't know really 'cos I was waiting for trial. It's all kind of strange for me."

"I was overwhelmed with happiness. I was just happy."

"Just make 'em aware – mine are just a year apart two boys and a girl. Let 'em know family's important – stick together. If they get in trouble family is the main stability in life."

"I'm afraid for my kids 'cos there's too much rubbish going on out there now. I just hope to do a good job now so they don't mess up in future."

"Now about coping on the out – say you got a daughter, a girl and a guy comes in – 17 with attitude - what would you do?"

"I wouldn't be happy at all but I'd make sure both of them was aware of what could happen if they start messing about."

"I think I'd have to be quite assertive. In my mind I couldn't trust him. You said he had attitude. I'd lock him off that's it. My daughter doesn't need people like that – people like me, really. You know what I mean? Like me really."

"I won't stop her seeing him. I wanna try and help her, but…at the end of the day at that age she gonna have to make her own life and learn. But I will try and steer her in the right direction. It's up to her if she wants to take advice at age 17/18 whatever. But I'd make sure she doesn't get pregnant if she doesn't want that."

"I'm just happy she's female because all the daughters in the family have made something of their lives and all the lads have just ended going off the rails, so I know she should… like…"

"What personal qualities have you got – when you get out – what are you going to offer your child?"

"Just love and money and be there for her."

"Um…awareness. I'm aware of how things were for me and I'm aware that if I don't do something to help my kids, you know – then things'll go wrong for them."

"I've got unconditional love for them no matter what and I'm gonna treat them – show 'em right from wrong – bring 'em up as best I can and just hope we make 'em a better person than what I was."

"Well, experience of life and crime and things like that. I can teach them not to do that. Go to school properly. I mean, I care a lot for them."

"I'll be there everyday taking them to school till they old enough to go themselves and letting them know how important it is to knuckle down and do the work."

"You see I can't read. I'd go to school and just be there."

Below are two poems written in the Swinfen Hall creative writing project, with writer in residence Maria Whatton. We are grateful to the authors, they know who they are.

I Despise The Lies.

I despise the lies my mother told
me when my father died.
Terrible deceiving lies, my
mother told me when my father died.
But when I heard the news of my
Father's death, I didn't cry.
I didn't shed a single tear and
sometimes I wonder why.
Maybe it's because somewhere deep inside I
believed what my
mother said, even though they
had to be lies.
She said, " your Daddy was a
bastard, he didn't care for you.
When did you ever see him?
When was he ever there for you?
And to this I would reply in a
smart boy tone,
He'd never come to this house,
cause you're always home."
And for that reply I'd take off
with a ringing in my ear, after
a slap off my lovely mother dear.

My Evaluation

There was no thought of contraception,
I was another unintentional conception, It was my
father's heated passion
Which led to my momma's impregnation,
There was no marriage certification,
Just the most evil combination…
Of lust and self-gratification,
Hot sex and lot's of perspiration,
My father's determination to reach ejaculation,
To plant the seed of Nathan….
Lord knows there was no intention.
After my momma's 9 months of anticipation,
There was another bastard born into the nation,
My father showed no appreciation,
Was I just a mere complication?
Momma showered me with attention,
And 100% devotion…
Even so, I was born into confusion,
What a fucked up situation.
Before long my father goes in a new direction,
This is no weak assumption,
My father went to find a new plantation
To plant the seed of Ashley…
Once again there was no intention,
For momma, another 9 months of anticipation,
Another baby showered with love and affection.
I look back in fascination,
3 kids, with just a mother showing dedication,
my apologies, I forgot to mention,
about 4 and a half years before my creation,
there was my brother Jason…
All men need to listen up and pay attention,
Because it's more than just copulation.

"I was in care from eleven years old and in a psychiatric ward from twelve. I was adopted and there was no communication – my sister was adopted separately. I get visits from my adopted parents and my girlfriend. I get a lot of help from them and I've got a job. I was influenced by a gang and got a reputation for street fighting. Your first few years change a lot of stuff. I've got an attachment disorder."

Support for young fathers?

"What kind of strategy do you need in prisons to deal with the emotional side of being a young father?"
Unless personal details are given, speakers are from Swinfen Hall.

"Someone to talk to instead of keeping it all to yourself inside. Someone there who understands – you can talk to. Someone to listen, not to do anything about it, just to listen."

"Someone who understands, who's been there, done that. Not necessarily who's been in jail, but someone who's a father who understands your point of view. 'Cos there's people on the wing here who you talk to - you can't really go into that…'cos they're just not interested."

"Someone with experience who's got a positive outlook, who's you know, been in your situation and who's come out of it with a positive outlook."

"I still feel that a parent needs their own self-esteem to deal with the role of being a parent – the full responsibility can be frightening and for some people it can be easier not to bother or make the effort. But you should let your feelings out and not be ashamed to cry. The course has helped me with these feelings. I think it should be available for more people. When I get out I hope to help others even in a small way. The staff are helping me get information together to possibly run a course in a local community centre. I know from me how much I didn't know and wished I had. There are lots of young people out there who have no idea how to be a parent or a partner. Maybe the schools should help more, I don't know."
J. is 24 and his daughters are 6 and 4 years old. He is serving 4 years in HMP Wolds.

So many issues…

"My worst moment was when I was 'phoned from hospital and told I had a son. It's not nice to be away from kids – they need both parents at home. She lives with her parents and I've not seen her since Christmas. Life changed when she was pregnant, and I tried to stay in, we had been together three years. We had no advice on contraceptives, I was frightened for the baby in hospital.
I've had no security in the people I knew. My Dad left when I was four and my step Dad left when I was twelve or thirteen years old. Three of my uncles have been in prison and I found out my Dad was in prison when I was fourteen. He was always in trouble with the old Bill. It would've helped if we could've gone and talked. We had been close but after I was fourteen we did not speak. I lived

at home but stayed at a friend's house for weeks on end. I was expelled from school. I've not been to school since I was eleven or twelve. I went out with my older brothers and uncles. This is my third sentence, my co-defendant is my girlfriend's brother. Things will be different when I go back. I'll have an apprenticeship course on release and I'll live with my Mum. She paid attention when we were little and she's been supportive. My kid will make a difference – my kid seeing me in here."

A. 17, in Portland. His son is seven months and his girlfriend is seventeen.

" I'm going to advanced foster parents and I'll get an allowance. Got a job lined up. it's a second chance - knew him from children's home. My father did not want to know. I got expelled from school at 8 years old. We never talked about my parents splitting up. I was in care from ten years old. If my girlfriend says 'I'm doing well really,' it makes me depressed. If she's depressed it makes me depressed. It's really hard to get everything into 5 minutes – really hard-everyone is waiting for the 'phone. It's really scary knowing that I have that responsibility, no other way now. It's really important the baby knows me. I'll always be there for him or her."

C.16 years and his girlfriend 17, expect a baby. He is in Portland.

"I was in care from eleven years old and in a psychiatric ward from twelve. I was adopted and there was no communication – my sister was adopted separately. I get visits from my adopted parents and my girlfriend. I get a lot of help from them and I've got a job. I was influenced by a gang and got a reputation for street fighting. Your first few years change a lot of stuff. I've got an attachment disorder. At fourteen I was fighting and I hit a boy with a metal bar.

I'm going to find my birth Mum though through an adoption agency. I'm going to be a Dad and find a Mum all in one hit! Mum was only thirteen years old when she had me. It's going to be strange for my girlfriend when I get out and the baby's due at anytime now. I've got 50 letters to send she may see along with poems I write her and shit. I don't know where to go for help… I would go to mates or parents."

B. 17, and girlfriend is 16, baby due at any time. Portland, serving a two month sentence.

"It's not nice being a Dad in prison. All I had on my mind was him. We were living together at my Mum's. My relationship with my Dad is better since I've been in prison – he visits, but I was twelve when my Mum and Dad split up. We went on holiday with Mum, and Dad had another woman in the house. We moved to a new area and I lost all my friends. It would have made a big difference if someone had supported the kids.

> "I don't want this life for my kids. Why should they suffer because of the stupid things I've done? I take my responsibility as a Dad much more seriously now, only I'm not there to do much about it, but I mean to be there for them."

My sister offered support. I was on a training course before and want to return to it. I'm missing the baby most and my mates I'm closest to. I thought the rewards would be better and didn't think twice about the consequences. Mum was working and it felt like she wasn't there for me. Kids need a mother and father talking to them and asking what my problems are. When she was at work she was ignoring me and so I started doing my own thing. A job I had lasted two weeks. But I've learned my lesson, it would break my heart to go to prison again. It would hurt me inside. My child would feel 'he is not there for me'. He loves attention and talk. I'll have to keep out of trouble – not easy in here. You can't tell your kids you love them enough."

R.18, has a baby of seven months. He is in Portland.

I was a young father...

"We had the first one when I was 18 years old and we are still together; we always wanted to have kids. I was there when the eldest and youngest were born, but I was inside for the middle girl. I wish I had been there but things worked out the way they did and I can't change it. I hope things work out better in future for all of us. Like most people I know I shouldn't have got into trouble, but I did. I didn't take things seriously when I was younger. I didn't understand what responsibility was really. I loved having the kids but didn't fully understand the responsibility. But I'm still pleased I had them with the same girl. I would say to other blokes, just realize what you're doing. I don't want this life for my kids. Why should they suffer because of the stupid things I've done? I take my responsibility as a Dad much more seriously now, only I'm not there to do much about it, but I mean to be there for them. I think most parents want to be – but things go wrong."

B, 26, HMP Kirklevington Grange, serving a four year sentence, three children aged 7,6,and 18 months.

Depression and missing family

"In here you have to get yourself a routine so you haven't time to think. In the daytime I haven't got time to think. It's in the night time when it all starts coming."

Psychological
problems

CHAPTER SEVEN - PSYCHOLOGICAL PROBLEMS

Psychological problems

"My Mum used to sit in a chair in the corner of the living room and just stare at the walls for ages."
K. 16, her Dad is inside.

"In the eight weeks my daughter was off work she had a mental breakdown and overdosed, she took off in her car one night and I couldn't find her, got her on her mobile and told her that I'd have to call the police which brought her to her senses and she came home. She had to have mental health involved." *Mother, whose son was sentenced to 2 years.*

"Bob suffers from Post Traumatic Stress Disorder from being in Bosnia, he has a drug problem too, at least he did have. He gets no counselling for the PTSD in there, he sees a psychologist once a week but he says that all she does is listen to him talk for an hour and that's it. Bob doesn't think that she's interested in what he's saying to her and what's going on in his head. This isn't his first time in prison but it's the first time since I've known him, we had been together for about 18 months before he went away, we didn't live together but we were seeing each other. I knew he'd get a prison sentence at court but the length of time was a shock - a great big shock, we never expected him to get that long. There was never any doubt that I'd stand by him. It was put over as a violent offence, he was a passenger in a stolen car being chased by the police and someone got hurt.

I've always smoked but I smoke more now, I'm on anti depressants now. My last visit was a disaster because we were put at the end of the room where the kids all play. It was so noisy that we couldn't hear ourselves think so we asked the SO if we could be moved. The SO got really nasty and insulting towards the both of us and Bob answered him back so he (SO) discontinued the visit, he stank of drink and was in a bad mood, his eyes were all red and angry. I wanted to tell him that I am a professional person – a nurse and that as far as intelligence goes I could wipe the floor with him but you can't do anything in that situation, they would have taken it out on Bob. It got really nasty, I told Bob to leave it – it doesn't matter but the SO was on a roll so they discontinued the visit and took him out without my having the chance to say goodbye. I was crying and couldn't stop crying and I felt so stupid.

I rang the wing that night, some of the staff there are OK, the officer said that Bob was alright, that he was behind his door…. What does that mean? He's behind his door and depressed and not talking to anybody, I worry about him all of the time. He only talks to me, he doesn't tell his Mum anything because he doesn't want to worry her and in front of his mates he acts all happy. I know about the listeners scheme and told Bob about it but he will not talk to anybody but me. I don't tell him my problems, he has enough to think about, I wrote to the governor about the visit but don't expect I will get an answer."
Dee 47, Dee's partner Bob received a five-year sentence, he has approximately. 1 year left to serve, she has two sons aged 19 and 21 years.

"I get some support from the probation and social services. I'm actually doing the course but I am only working with the social worker. I'm the only one doing it that I know of. They say it is because I am willing to start to understand my husband and what he has done and how he can change with help. We look at everything in a circle – the offence, the thoughts before, the thoughts during the offence – it's basically what he is doing. I find it hard and draining and mind blowing. I've questioned myself so much. So I suppose this course is some form of support if you want to look at it like that. I am wiling to do anything to help him. I have my family and they are great. It must be worse if you don't have anyone to share with. All too often partners are just left alone physically and emotionally because of the crime, people do not want to know you and that is not a nice feeling. Partners need support. I go to bed early after East Enders. That's when I write to him. It sounds mad but I feel if I go to bed early, time will go quicker. It's hard to write letters now what can you say after 15 months? It feels like a lifetime. When I think about the course it's better than nothing. But I do keep asking why should I have to do it – but the social workers keep reminding me that I want to help him – so I keep on with it. I want him to come back. I want him home. I know it will never be the same. How can it be? I have a niece who stays with me to keep me company and I can talk to her, which is good. I sometimes wish I could get drunk and forget all about it, but then I will have to wake up the next morning and feel even worse so what is the point? I am on anti-depressants. We are worried about what he will do when he comes out. He won't be able to go back to his job. All his pensions are frozen till he is 65. So we might start to have a life one day." *C. mother of two teenager sons.*

"When my brother was first arrested it really didn't sink in - I was in pure shock. I kept thinking it was all lies by the police, that he must have been innocent. I just didn't know what to believe. It was a really hard time. I think that the first time it really hit me properly was when he went to court. It was so difficult seeing him there. I just kept thinking that he would get off, that y'know he would be coming back home with us. He hadn't got any previous conviction, I thought there was no chance would he get a sentence. When the judge gave him a sentence I just burst into tears, I was absolutely devastated. I didn't even get any time off work because I was so convinced that my brother would get off. I did go to work but I couldn't face anyone. Me and my Mum worked at the same place and she stayed but I had to go home. After the court hearing, I was off work for three months, suffering from depression. I just couldn't get over what had happened. Although some times it was really tough I was still feeling really depressed and eventually I took an overdose 'cos I just couldn't cope with things more. I didn't tell him at the time, I just couldn't cope with it all, I was so angry at him."
Kerrie 24, whose brother was sent to prison for 2 years.

"Eventually I took an overdose 'cos I just couldn't cope with it anymore. I didn't tell him at the time. I was so angry at him."

"He had been depressed for quite some time before things went wrong. He got drunk and just lost it. He shouldn't have gone to prison – even the staff say that. But he did and we both say something good has come from something bad. He needed help – he was depressed. We kept going to the GP but he said therapy was expensive and just gave tablets, which didn't help. Prison has been good for him. He gets help inside and they have set up help for when he comes home. He has been seeing a psychiatrist, which has helped him and will continue to see him when he gets out.

I don't get any help from any professionals. Nobody has really offered me any except my family. My GP wanted to give me anti-depressants, but I didn't want that. He really needed prison to help him; I suppose we can talk like this because he only got a short sentence. I can't imagine what it must be like when someone gets years to serve. Before he went to court, the barrister said he could have been looking at six years but he only got months. He was ill; he was/is a genuine case. I know people must say that to you often, but it's true. His circumstances were making him ill. He worries about everything.

We asked about his sentence before he went to court and I was honest with him. I didn't know if I would be able to cope on my own working full time and a single parent for about six years. That was a terrible time not knowing, but once he got his time things did improve. It proved he really did need help. The staff are great. I've written to my local MP and the Governor at Durham, thanking them for all the help they have given my husband. He has a good relationship with the staff and in a strange way he will miss them – they have been good to him.

He has said he would like to go back and visit people that don't have any friends. He is a good man and I'm pleased he has been given some help. I don't like to visit but it's easier now and especially since we know it's coming to an end. I've kept busy. I've had no choice really: work and my daughter fill my time. But I do go out one night a week with friends; these are the friends that have stood by me and helped us to get through it.

Most people know he's in prison and most people feel sorry that he was ill and should have gone to hospital. But they are pleased he is coming home. There are the odd ones that don't speak or give you strange looks but are they worth knowing? How do these people know it will never happen to them? I don't bother about these people. I've told my husband that real friends have stuck by us and will always be there – they are the people who matter to me.

Our daughter misses him but it would have been worse if I wasn't around. Before all of this happened, due to his depression he didn't and couldn't do much, he just sat around most of the time. So it tended to be me that did most things, but she does ask about him and talks to him on the phone. He should be home just after her fourth birthday, so she knows that's her present. He does miss her and he says he has been a bad Dad and partner by going to prison. That's something we need to work on and talk about. I know he hasn't been a bad Dad, but he needs to feel better about himself and change. I've had to be tougher.

Christmas was a bad time. She couldn't understand why Dad wasn't with us but it's only one day – he has the rest of his life with us. He always asks about her when I visit and when he 'phones he loves talking to her. But the staff help him and talk sense to him. It's strange but I really don't know all of the details – what happened to him to do what he did. I know we'll have to talk about it, but now he is getting help it will be easier. I am nervous about him coming home. I've had to get used to him being away. I still work and will continue to do so. Things will be different. I'll still go out, but not as often. I'm sure he's nervous about coming home and seeing everyone. I just want him back and to get on with our lives. My family will continue to support us. My Dad went to visit him with me early on, but he got angry. He couldn't cope with all the searching. He hasn't been back but he speaks to him often when he 'phones. They all feel he was ill and needed help, but it took prison not the NHS to help to sort him out. He has done maths and computer courses, which he would never have done. He has been encouraged by the staff in a way I couldn't do.

I'm lucky our daughter is young. My family look after her or she is at playgroup when I visit. I have to take time off work if I visit during the week. That can be a pain sometimes but it is manageable. Durham is not too far from home – at least I haven't got miles to travel like some. But the visits are hard, everyone looking at each other, wondering who has done what. I don't want to know about others. The staff are great and make it easier, but it's still very strange – it's not something I could ever say I'm used to. But I couldn't miss [a visit] - we need to talk. He needs to know what my life is like, just as I need to understand his life at the moment. We are not going to rush anything when he gets home. He hopes to do some voluntary work so we are keeping an open mind."
JW.

The human cost – ripples through the generations.

"I worry about the stability of my child sometimes as she suffers nightmares and often calls out 'Daddy' during the night. I worry that she's having nightmares about me being dead or hurt somewhere 'cos I'm not there. It's hard for me when my girlfriend tells me stuff like that."
D. 20, HMP YOI Brinsford, his daughter knows him well. She is three and he sees her twice a week. They have told her he is in hospital. He makes a considerable effort to write and speak to her as well as the visits. He makes her little gifts also.

"The worst thing about being away from my child is not being able to see her whenever I want, her birthday was the worst time." *Prison father.*

"One of the kids has Downs syndrome. She's been in care for years. My youngest lad has a learning problem and attention deficit syndrome. I have a sixteen year old girl but no contact with her. My first baby died. He would have been twenty-four years old. My oldest girl has two kids in care and one baby going to be adopted."

Mother 41, in Low Newton .

"This isn't the first time he's been to prison, it's the third or fourth time, he's been in prison since he was 16, he hasn't had a Christmas out since he was 16, that's why he's gutted this time cos he won't be out in time."

"We all get letters from him, (Dad, inside) but my older brother's angry and he doesn't want to know. He thinks that Mum has had to go through all that, she wouldn't go out the house because of the dirty looks and her drinking, she shut herself off, she was drinking because of him, when he says we are in the wrong we think, you did all this, you did worse. He hates being wrong. I wasn't around to see it all I didn't stick around; I went to live with my boyfriend. I came round now and again but everyone was always upset and I couldn't handle it. I was stealing things for my boyfriend, I don't know why I did it now, it's in the past, and he's in prison now. I went to court on my birthday, they gave me youth offending team 'cos I am pregnant. They've been pretty good and are helping me through the pregnancy. I don't really see them much anymore. They put a parenting order on my Mum where she has to attend classes to learn how to be a parent, but she hasn't been yet 'cos of all her other problems. Really, my Mum got done for what I did wrong which wasn't fair cos I wasn't living with my Mum at the time. I'm living back at home now.

Christmas will be hard but we've handled it this long we can handle it for another couple of months after Christmas when he comes home. To me, both my Dad's and my boyfriend's sentences have gone quick. My sister has gone out of order 'cos of this, she won't do nothing my Mum tells her. The only person she listens to is me really, apart from telling her to go to school. I had to pretend to cry to make her come in the house. She always looks up to me, which is why I moved back and home and tried to be good again. I think that the situation and me being pregnant has made me grow up, I haven't got a choice have I? I can see now where I went wrong. I used to think I was in the right and everyone else is wrong and now you learn to live with life don't you. The only thing I'm worried about is that when he (father) comes home he won't let me stay here while they move away, but he's got to let go sometimes, my brother and his girlfriend had a baby and moved away at 15. To him I've always been the little baby, I can't do anything wrong to him. I mean when I stole money from him, Mum was going to call the police but he wouldn't let her. But he's got to think about the other little ones now. I want to stay for when my boyfriend gets out, I don't want to move away, I was born here, I don't ever want to leave. I get on well with my boyfriend, well we have our ups and downs, his Mum and me don't get on but I get on with his Dad. He won't get tagging 'cos he's been on it before and he broke it every night. I thought it was a stupid idea cos it was for the evenings but he was done for thieving from shops so why didn't they put him on tag in the day, it was ridiculous. Probation won't let him have one again cos they can't trust him. This isn't the first time he's been to prison, it's the third or fourth time, he's been in prison since he was 16, he hasn't had a Christmas out since he was 16, that's why he's gutted this time 'cos he won't be out in time. He used to take heroin but I told him if he takes that crap again, that's it. Next time it won't be young offenders." *K, 16.*

"I feel different compared to the other women as my children are grown up and I have grandchildren. The women here are all much younger. Things are difficult keeping contact with everyone as my husband and son are in prison in cells next to each other. We do get inter prison visits but they are few and far between and very strained. I am here because I took the blame for my son – but what else can a mother do? My husband didn't know anything about it so he got involved and ended up in prison.

My mother has just gone into hospital so I don't know what's happening there. My daughter and sisters should keep me up to date but things are difficult between us all. I have a sister dying of cancer and I have been allowed to see her but that was the most awful time, and I don't know if I'll see her again. I have seen my daughter a few times but we don't get on very well. She is looking after my other son who is brain damaged from a car accident. He has a poor memory and asks for me all the time. I feel I've put a lot onto my daughter and I should be there for them. My other son is awaiting a court hearing and will probably go to prison. The whole family is falling apart. I spend my money on 'phone cards to keep contact with my daughter to see how my son is or what needs to be sorted out. I'm still the mother - but not. I don't see my grandchildren as my son's ex won't let me. I feel desperate some days. My father died recently and I still feel I'm getting over that. How am I going to make up for lost time?"
S. 46, serving a four year sentence in Low Newton. Mother of four children and two grandchildren.

"I like being at Nanny's because I see all my cousins and that, we all knock around together, me, my brother and my cousins. We keep the dogs down here; we've got dogs and bantam hens. My mother hates the dogs and definitely won't let them in the house – definitely not! she put a sign on our back door, it says the dogs are alright but beware of the kids. Our Josh is quieter than me so everybody always blames me when things go wrong, he's got an innocent face so he gets away with everything. I got arrested off the Busies before, they took my 'photo and fingerprints for breaking into a garage, my Dad went mental, my uncle Keith came down the Busy Station and got me 'cos my Dad didn't want to come down 'cos if they knew I was his son they would have probably tried to blame me for things. I'm saving up to get a little wagon or a tidy van so I can go out working when I'm 17, my Dad's gonna help me to get the wagon. Me and Josh like to be at Nanny's, we go to Dad and Jenny's sometimes for our dinner, Jenny makes nice dinners, she's OK but her son is a right pain in the arse, he's always moaning. I don't know if Jenny likes us or if she gives us our dinner because Dad tells her to. I only remember seeing Dad in prison once, my mother was a bit of a bitch to him I think and didn't want us to see him, I don't

"I would have preferred to have been locked away saved from this... He's had a lot of support."

K. 38.

"My daughter and me came to the court on the day of sentence, but my daughter was in juvenile court at the same time 'cos she'd got into trouble at the same time as this was all going on which was awful."

remember all that much but I know I would go to jail to see him if I could. I don't want to go to jail, no way, but I don't think there's that much wrong with going to jail, loads of people go don't they? My Dad wouldn't like it if I went. Dad says that Mam is a good mother and brought us up properly, he says that they couldn't get on but she's a good mother. I like being at Nanny's because she doesn't give you grief and she buys meat for the dogs. I don't like school it's a waste of time for me, I want to work for my uncle Keith, Josh is clever but he likes to be with me, we'll work together, we do now, we put the bills through the doors to try and get work for plastic guttering. I want to keep out of trouble, Dad says that jail is for mugs and idiots and you're better off working for a living, I don't drink or smoke and drugs are for idiots, I go to the gym and I'm fit and can look after myself."
Little Jack 14.

"The girls are no bother but the lad who's 14 years is always in trouble. He's spent more time in the cop-shop than I have."
E 46, HMP Kirklevington Grange four year sentence.

Karen 38

"Don't know where to start really; basically it's just been hell. I got a 'phone call saying 'Mum quick Dad's just killed someone.' I got a lift into town and went looking for him, someone told me that he was at the police station, but he was at a different one. I found my daughter 'cos she was involved. A lot of it's a blur really as I've tried to block it out. They didn't let me see him until the evening. He was remanded straight away, sent to Winson Green straight away. It was like a complete whirlpool, totally gob smacked, I had lots of questions via the police. My husband was a mess. I didn't understand what was going on straight away just that he was at the police station and that it was serious offence. They had lots of questions for me, such as what has gone on in the past. I wasn't impressed with the way it was all done. They didn't search the other guy's house for the evidence that was there. I knew that in the mean time people had cleared out his flat before the police could get there. At that stage he was looking at attempted murder. I was totally out of it, too much to take in. Even now when he's so close to coming home, there's still a lot of stuff that is still playing on my mind, that's the reason why I ended up in psychiatric care last week. All this stuff still whirling round in my head, I've got to have counselling now.
My daughter and me came to the court on the day of sentence, but my daughter was in juvenile court at the same time 'cos she'd got into trouble at the same time as this was all going on which was awful. He got 2 years, which was a real shock, but the judge said he'd never seen a case like this before. He was taken to Winson Green. It was horrible seeing him after he'd been sentenced. Like I said it was a relief for him getting the 2 years but there's a lot of blame. He said to me

'if you hadn't done such and such, then it wouldn't have happened'. There were questions between us to deal with but wasn't anytime to sort them out before he was sentenced. I blamed myself at first, lots of emotional turmoil. Right up until about 2 months ago he blamed me until I found out what he'd been up to. There was already lots of pressures on the marriage which lead up to the crime which I couldn't even sort out before he went away. It took around nine months after he went away to try and get it sorted out; we spent a lot of time with the Chaplain. I found it hard to go and visit him, I don't like it. The first time was very emotional, I'm not up on prisons and I didn't realise just how restrictive it was going to be. We were both crying most of the way through the first visit. He kept saying he was sorry at first, but then he had time to think especially with him being on 23 hour lock up which is when I started getting these negative letters. He was then put on suicide watch a couple of times 'cos he didn't think he could get through it. 'Cos there was no communication we just couldn't sort anything out. I felt really cut off; letters weren't enough to sort everything out. The first letters were quite harsh; with stuff he was feeling and now touch wood we are on the mend.

On top of that I've had a load of grief with my daughter who has been in a load of trouble, in court for burglary. My kids knew all of what was going on. What I've done is tell the kids before they had chance to hear it off anyone else. It came out in the paper, front page. They were actually asked in court to be lenient for the children's sake but they didn't bother, I wasn't impressed with that at all. I had a lot of backlash off his family. I shut myself away, I didn't like going out, partly cos of other people in the town. There were dirty looks and snide remarks when I walked past. There was a lot of blame, which came on to me from the kids for their Dad being in prison, but once they found out more it wasn't so bad. His Mum has started to talk to me but only since people went to her and told her the truth.

I could go for so long and then I'd shut myself upstairs in my room. I turned to drink in a big way as well; I'm getting counselling now. I just couldn't handle it so I tried to shut it all out. Lots of times I wanted to ring someone but thought I could handle it but obviously I couldn't do it on me own. SHARP is my only support, as I haven't got any family. In the beginning I blamed myself for it all but now I've learned more and realised it's not all my fault and also the kids do need me to keep going, if I fail then I've got no one. The visits were better at the Winson Green; our visits were nearly 2 hours long. At Featherstone they cut them short, sometimes we only have an hour. In some ways it's put a wedge between the kids and us. For what my husband and me have done to the kids and got rid of the trust. They don't know whether to believe whether we'll stay together

"I could go for so long and then I'd shut myself upstairs in my room. I turned to drink in a big way as well; I'm getting counselling now. I just couldn't handle it so I tried to shut it all out. Lots of times I wanted to ring someone but thought I could handle it but obviously I couldn't do it on me own."

"I feel that my punishment has been worse than that of my husbands. He has had a lot of support, some people even praised him for what he did, he's had work, made friends, life out here just seems to be one long struggle,

when he comes home and everything will be alright. But in other ways, the kids and me have got stronger together, but they still have a lot of questions they want to ask him when he comes home. He knows that and he's quite worried about it, he'll be quite unsettled when he gets back anyway, he's quite concerned about what he's done. When my 15-year-old daughter left home, it made it worse, she was getting in a lot of trouble, her boyfriend is actually a heroin addict, and she was stealing things for him. I got another shock when I was told I'd have to attend parenting classes.

We are going to move away when he gets back, there's a lot of bad memories here I don't want to risk anything, I don't know whether my husband will be able to cope being here. If he gets Tag he will be out Christmas Eve but he might not, we don't want to know much about it in case we build our hope up for him coming out for Christmas. I have worries about when he comes out, with the whole trust thing; we've got to learn to trust each other again. I'm going to be on edge if he goes out anywhere, but he has assured me he will stay at home 24-7 if needs be to get me to trust him again. We want to make a fresh start. The kids are very much for it apart from my one daughter who wants to stay put. I'm coping better in some ways but not others, I'm trying to keep off the booze, Christmas will, be difficult 'cos I don't want to build the kid's hopes up if he's not out by then, that will be another bridge to across.

Sometimes that last bit's the worst bit, I'm sure it will go slower My other kids have all rebelled. My one daughter keeps running away from home or won't take her insulin. I don't like my daughters' boyfriend and don't make no secret of it. In some ways I feel that I have bore the brunt of what's happened. I feel that my punishment has been worse than that of my husbands'. He has had a lot of support, some people even praised him for what he did, he's had work, made friends, life out here just seems to be one long struggle, I've got work and this house. My personal opinion is that I would have preferred to have been locked away safe from all of this. In another way I feel like it's all my own fault. I feel like I deserve this somehow, I didn't deserve how severe it went, but I did make a big mistake. I don't like what we both did to the kids.

Last couple of months it's been even harder to be close to the kids, they've been really naughty. My one daughter has had the police round here and if she causes any more trouble she'll be put in a cell. They watch me cry and they just look at me now and just let me get on with it. I wish more than anything to be able to wipe the past out I think what got to me the most was the court, not being able to speak to him. I asked to speak to him, it was just a no but they never say why. At the moment I'm looking at it that my husband can take over the kids for a bit to give me a break from the kids.

I think the younger kids will calm down when he's back but not with the older ones 'cos they've got so many questions. My eldest son's really angry and had a go at me. I think there will be a lot of friction. I think he'll find it difficult to answer the questions but he will... they might not like the answers though. He was quite close with the boys (19 & 17) but he did admit that he didn't have that much time for them. He's written it all down. I think that spending a night in psychiatric care has made me realise that I need to be stronger as I saw in other people how I could be and I decided that I don't want to go down that road."
Karen 38.

A life disconnected from anything before

"One of the worst things about it all was the isolation, we had moved to this house fairly recently before my husband went to prison so my friends or family didn't live locally anymore. At one point my Mum came to stay but that actually made things much harder for me to cope with. I found it vital to be able to get into a routine in order to keep going. He 'phoned me everyday, we had good communication with each other and we tried really hard to stay close. When it all happens it is devastating at first, you just don't know how you are going to get through it all, but you just have to have tunnel vision to cope with things. We were lucky to have such a strong marriage." *Elise 35.*

Do men and women react differently?

"It wasn't so bad for the man like, but how I saw it affected the mother, she fell apart, I had to take her to the doctor's, in fact she's still on tablets now, she just couldn't cope, and now she's having counselling as well and this is since he's come out like.

The way I tried to look at it was as if he was in the army, and come home on leave and then gone back. But his mother was like 'he's gonna be locked up again'. This was the hard part. He didn't want to see his Mum upset, and that's why he wanted to go back and finish his time. I think it did help pretending he was in the army. It must be worst for married people who have children and take them, because it's so hard. I don't think it's so hard for the men like, we seem to be able to cope like, but for the women, it so hard to see them in prison and then just walk out. I thought it was going to be quite a lot better when he got out but she keeps making excuses all the time. Before it was when he's off tagging it'll get better, now it's like when he's off probation it will be better, I've asked her, well what will it be after that?"
Ken 65, his son served 15 months in prison.

"The problem came when I didn't want to go back to work, couldn't face anybody, people were coming up to me and saying they were sorry and me and my daughter just broke down, my daughter walked out of work, she was off for eight weeks."

Anon mother – her son was sentenced to 2 years.

"It did worry me at first, people ignoring me. I just know why they did. I mean, I felt really ashamed of what he'd done. I've tried to get over that with time."

Flesh and Blood

"When I told my Dad, he told me that he expected my brother to get a sentence. I felt hurt by that 'cos he had neglected us. I'm quite close to my brother these days but he has been back in court since and I don't go anymore, I think that it's best that way. My Mum and my brother get on better now. I feel like I'm stuck in the middle. I give money now to try and keep the peace. He is back in prison now but I try and let it go over my head 'cos I can't cope with it. SHARP helped me a lot, I felt lost without their help .I think it's a different experience for every family, so it's difficult to generalise what kind of help is needed. Me and my brother don't have a very good relationship but at the end of the day he is flesh and blood so you carry on."
Kerrie 24, her brother received a prison sentence.

"It's a lot of pressure trying to pay his debts off but it will be all over on Friday when the house sale goes through, that's where all my money's gone. My son has his own home, he had a mortgage at 18, I've been renting it out for him so when he comes out he'll have a home to go to. He was so stupid, just got himself into so much debt. But at the end of the day he is my son. I don't feel that its' my duty to do so but if all the debt isn't cleared by the time he comes out then he'll just be back to square one. I'm angry for what's done. I'm angry. I'm not angry for me paying out the money. If a friend of mine was in the same situation and I'd got the money, I think, I'd do the same for them. It did worry me at first, people ignoring me. I just know why they did. I mean, I felt really ashamed of what he'd done. I've tried to get over that with time. I think that people thought he is a nice lad, he was a nice lad, but he just got caught up in things that he shouldn't have done, with people he shouldn't have done. I think the situation would have got much worse if I hadn't had anything to do with it."
Jean 46, has lost her home and her marriage has broken up over her son's crimes. He is 21.

"I couldn't bring his girlfriend and the baby here anyway, I have to get somebody else to bring me. They're his family really but she's had enough, don't suppose I can blame her, she should have her life, but it's hard to go against them when they're your flesh and blood."
Danny has three sons in prison – all through heroin. He is severely disabled but visits all of them; one of his sons is a father.

"You hate the deeds that he's done but you love the child, Owen has been to prison twice, this time it was for something he didn't do, the last time it was for something he had done. He got five years and had just lost his father, he got so long because he used a toy gun, he had problems with drugs, the sentence was ludicrous, it didn't match the crime, he and his friend were out of their brains on drugs. The policeman even told me it wasn't Bonny and Clyde – more like Laurel and Hardy but that the consequences would be awful, he said that he felt sorry for me and Owen."
Lorna 54, supporting her son Owen 28.

Dealing with a painful past

Wooden Bars by P.G. from Feltham

"It's happening again. What can I do? I'm locked in: besides, he's much bigger than me. It doesn't happen all the time. Sometimes I lie here quiet, hoping they would come to see me. If they did they would get me a drink and go, but I've got used to it now and it doesn't bother me. Anyway, I've been quiet for a long time now. I've learned to keep the noise down. It doesn't help my situation. Anyway, I've been quiet for a long time now and often wonder if I have a voice. If I have, it's never heard, so what's the point?
I awoke shivering the other night. One blanket is not so nice. I can't complain to my superiors 'cos they never listen. No time for me, and if they have it's just a front to cover their backs.

You know, I'd like to move from this room. It's damp, cold, infested with ants and it smells. I've not had a change of clothes sincer, er some time in Julember and I could do with a warm drink, but till then I'll just lie and dream. When I dream everything's nice. I'm free. It's sunny. Dad's got his arm around Mum, which is weird to see. It's normally with a new woman. I try to speak, but silence.

In my dreams Dad is nice to Mum. But as I said that's dreams and dreams are all I've got. I guess mine's of freedom.

I hate having a lock on the door. It feels all closed in and I find it hard to breathe. But it has a good side – keys. When I hear keys I get all excited. It gives me a sense of freedom 'cos one day they may be for me, to let me go. But each time it's pure disappointment. I sometimes wonder if I'm too old for my body, or I'm growing too quick, but only time will tell. These bars are cold and I feel weak and tired. Just as I slowly drift away, a sound catches my attention. It's the keys. The door flies open and a woman appears. She seems familiar, but in the distance of my mind I knew her. It was Mum.

She leaned over my bed, lifting me from my wooden barred cot. She was crying, saying sorry. I wanted to say something, but couldn't I tried to put some words together but all I could manage was 'Mum'. It was a big step for me as I'm not even 2 years old yet."

"I don't want my daughters to go through the pain and loss I've been through. My mother walked out on the family when I was a child. My father found it difficult coping with work and childcare. I was looked after by my aunt and uncle. However from an early age I was abused sexually by my uncle. I worry that history will repeat itself."

Val 26, Low Newton 6 months sentence.

"I didn't have a good childhood. I was abused physically and emotionally, but somehow nothing happened about it. It's only now that I've had the chance to deal with it. Prison has helped me in that way. I've worked things through with the counsellor. But it's still very real and painful to me. That's why I want a proper family. Mine wasn't. My parents split up. I can't understand why people repeat what has happened to them as a child. I want to be the opposite of what my parents were. I don't bother much with them these days. My girlfriend's family are really close to me and like what I want for my girls. I was there for the birth for both of them. Couldn't believe it. Very emotional. It changed me in a way. My girlfriend is very supportive. I'm sure we'll get through this. I hope to get moved to a Category D prison so I can get home visits. I haven't told my girls I'm in prison. Their school knows but they don't. Because they're young it's easier, they think I'm at work because I'm a welder and I show them things I make. I still think a parent needs their own self-esteem to deal with the role of being a parent. The full responsibility can be frightening and for some people it can be easier not to bother. But you should let your feelings out and not be ashamed to cry. When I first came to prison, to be honest I dropped the father role. I thought I would never be able to be part of their lives or be effective in any way to them as a father. When they were babies I used to love feeding them and doing all the things you do. But once I came in here I lost it. I thought I had lost it for good. But I started thinking and working through my past. It helped me. I think doing the parenting course helped me more than anything. It made me realise that I did have a role in their lives and it was important for me to keep the contact no matter how. It was essential to keep the relationship going. The course has helped me with these feelings. When I get out I hope to help others, even in a small way. The staff are helping me get information together to possibly run a course in the local community centre where I live. I know from me how much I didn't know and wished I had. I wish there had been someone to contact to get help." *Jaykay 24, HMP Wolds, 4 years. Served 17 months.*

"I feel so much guilt about my sister looking after my child. There's a lot of pressure from the family. I know I've done wrong but I didn't know what else to do. My daughters are separated, one lives with her Dad. She wants to stay with her Dad. She is happy and settled with him and his new wife so it would be wrong of me to move her. I hope people can understand it isn't that I don't love her, but it would be selfish of me to move her. I've only seen my eldest daughter three times in a year. I know I'm missing out on their little lives. I don't want my daughters to go through the pain and loss I've been through. My mother walked out on the family when I was a child. My father found it difficult coping with work and childcare. I was looked after by my aunt and uncle. However from an early age I was abused sexually by my uncle. I worry that history will repeat itself." *Val 26 ,Low Newton 6 months sentence.*

"His emotions are very sensitive now, he's been clean of drugs for four years and is really trying to out the past behind him, but you can't always can you? He has had to fight so hard to have access to his little girl. He took his ex-girlfriend to court and had the whole of his past dragged out there to be able to see his daughter for four hours each week. We are a strong family now though, and we cope."
Mother of twenty four year old son, ex- heroin addict, now released.

"I got married for the wrong reason. I shouldn't have but I just did it. It just happened I was pregnant. Everyone in our place got married. I didn't bother with school. I have five kids but I don't see them. How can I tell them the drugs come first? I've had a drug problem for years. They've seen me do heroin and everything. I want to tell them the truth but can't. I wasn't happy at home, my Dad hated me. I was just a bastard to him. He left my Mam, he was a womaniser. I can't talk to my Mam – our life was always bad. My eldest brother sexually assaulted me but nobody did anything about it. I hate him for doing it. I don't want my kids to have that. Most of my kids are grown up. My younger ones are by another man. He used to beat me up. I went to live in a bed and breakfast after that, but he knew where I was. When my hormones went all to pot I just took drugs. It was the only way for me. Prison is helping me stay off drugs."
C. 41, Low Newton TC unit. Serving a three year sentence, five children.

Drugs and all that goes with addiction

Sue was with her ex-partner since schooldays and has recently split from him. He has served several prison sentences. He is a heroin addict. Sue did a late degree and now helps to run a support group.

"I told the children he was working away. As they got older, I don't know what ages they were really, they started working things out for themselves, I wanted them to know the truth then, I didn't want it all coming back on me, so I was completely honest with them then. My partner thought I was trying to turn them against him but I said no, I wanted them to know the truth and they could make their own minds up about stuff when they were older, and that's the way it worked out really. They still see their Dad, I had endless nights worrying about my daughter because she's the soft one, and I've done it, I've given him money and stuff, kept letting him come back into our lives, but she's strong and she's the one who speaks her mind about his lifestyle. He was in prison in France last year and she was doing all the ringing round it's not fair on her, she was supporting him. If he turns up at our door now she gives him ciggies and things. I never took the kids to see him in prison when they were young, he was only ever in short times and I said he was working away, yes, I lied to them, but when they were older I come clean. The biggest feeling I've got of Mike, was being in jail

"The biggest feeling I've got of Mike was being in jail myself – he would go out to score, I wanted to go after him, stop him, but the kids were in bed, I couldn't leave them, I couldn't stop him, I was in jail myself, pulling my hair out, I wasn't on the 'phone or anything so I couldn't even ask anyone to come over."

myself – he would go out to score, I wanted to go after him, stop him, but the kids were in bed, I couldn't leave them, I couldn't stop him, it was like I was in jail myself, pulling my hair out, I wasn't on the 'phone or anything so I couldn't even ask anyone to come over. The stigma I felt was unbelievable, I met his probation officer later, when I started doing voluntary work, I was studying at the time and that was my way out I suppose, I remember thinking she (prob. Officer) must be thinking, what is she doing here? I felt crap. I did tell my bosses in social services about things but where I worked in the city, no one knew me. I nearly died when I saw her. Colleagues - I didn't tell them, told no one in University. Discussions there were real for me. My son is very quiet, he gets embarrassed about his Dad, you have to draw things out of him, and he doesn't enter into any conversation about him. When he (son) started secondary school he sat on the field with his new school friends and said my Dad's on drugs, I asked why he'd told them that he said well, if they're ever walking down the road with me and see him they'll know anyway so I just wanted it out in the open. My kids don't talk about it, they don't see him that much now, I know he loves them and he's mostly kept contact with them but he doesn't really know what being a Dad is, he's not a good Dad, he just does what fits in with his situation. I think my kids are OK, but, do they tell me what they really think? I don't know. Now I have a job working with drug users, Mike says he's done me a favour – given me a career Ha Ha, he says that he knew the kids were always OK because I'm a good mother, takes the worry off him doesn't it? How does he know I'm a good mother, he's never been there?" *Sue 36, her ex-partner has served several sentences. they have a daughter 17 and a son 14.*

"We were together about eight months in all, he moved up here to live with me, he started using again, I wasn't stupid, I'd worked with users, I knew he was using again. I knew he'd had problems with drugs before and his problems with addictions had never been addressed either, not the whole time he was inside. He went to London to see his sister one day, about eighteen months ago it was now, I knew he was going to visit his sister but what he hadn't told me was that he had committed two armed robberies before he came to live with me." *Gina 31, her partner was given a life sentence.*

"I never expected my husband to leave me 'cos I wanted to stand by my son. Not only that but he became really vindictive about it and turned his children against me and took the house away from me; he really didn't want to know anything about it. But at the end of the day he would have done the same thing for any of his children. I think that hurt more than anything. He became very jealous when I was trying to get my son off drugs as I would go and stay over at my son's house to make sure he didn't take anything and to nurse him. I didn't stay every night, as sometimes my Dad would go. It was only a couple of nights a

"I had to give my baby out to my Mum with the laundry when she was 6 weeks old, but my Mum was also an addict."

Young mother in Holloway at the time.

week unless I knew he was going through a really bad stage then I wouldn't like my Dad to have to see what he was like, 'cos it was frightening and I preferred to be there for him. It wouldn't have been fair on my Dad to see it. My son's had a lot of support, he really has, more support than I had! But everything that has happened has broke my marriage up, I've lost my home, I've no money and my son's in prison, nothing will ever be the same again. My husband wants to get back together again but he doesn't want to know my son, so we could never get back together as it would be a problem, I've had no support from him at all. I think now that he does realise that he's done the wrong thing but it's too late. He has spoken to him on the phone and asked him how he was but that was it."

Jean 45, has paid off her son's debts and lost her home and marriage. Her son is 21 and serving a sentence.

Addiction in the family

"My mother's a manageable addict - always has been. My daughter's seen me right down and picked myself up got clean and got a job and a house. I've also gone right down again. I do think regular contact with a child makes them feel you care. But a lot of women didn't want to put their children through the security searches and the wrench of anguish when you say goodbye after each visit. Also one or two people can ruin it for everybody else if they're bringing drugs in on a child in their clothing or toys. Imagine how the kid feels being used? But it could mean visits cancelled at the last minute and your family's come all the way and are waiting. The tension can be terrible among the women when a thing like this happens. Visiting arrangements aren't good although I know they have to have security. The woman should work on her self esteem or the child will pick up anything from the parent. It will cling to you – he can feel it. What's important is acceptance around yourself and your behaviour. You're throwing out an aura – if you're not alright in here – it's gonna throw the whole structure. I've learned it's you changing, the way you carry yourself you automatically attract different people into your life. You've got to learn to accept yourself even if you're smashed to pieces and think you're no good. When you're an addict, structure is important. Like a college course... voluntary work or something, otherwise the addict in your head gets to you. When my daughter was a baby I had to get the drugs just to be able to cope. I wasn't choosing between her and the drugs. You feel inadequate with a child. I felt it's driving me mad, I feel I can't cope. It would help if there was somewhere they could go to meet other young mothers. It's how you speak to the child. If you've been brought up by people who tell you you're stupid and no good – you believe it. You need to learn how to cope when your child is misbehaving and not learn the bad way to talk to kids. Like if I said 'Look at my hair – I look a mess' – my mother would say 'Who's gonna look at you anyway?' It's about the affirmation you give. My daughter 'phones me if she is pissed off. I give her a lot of affirmation. I ring her and tell her how much I love her. What's important for everyone that takes drugs, is - before – you got to look at the damage and repair from before. I know quite a few people who think they had a good upbringing, but they wouldn't be on drugs if there wasn't something before they went on drugs. Many addicts lived with violence or were carers (looking after their parents) or in destructive relationships.

"I want my son to have a chance. I love him and want to be there for him after all the crap he has had. I 'phone him every day. I have a massive fear he'll end up like me."

C. 35 years HMP Kirklevington Grange his son is 16.

We attract people same as we are. Even as adults… we still want it - affirmation from our parents. My Mum hasn't got a clue about co-dependency and how damaging it can be. It was one of my big issues. I looked at my behaviour. I have boundaries. I'm learning to deal with it. She's so dependent on a man – an abusive man. With other women sometimes with kids, some have limitations on them and can't contact them. A good social worker and care team is essential. You've really got to be a strong person to put your case across and say I've put the drugs down. I'm dealing with my behaviour. Some kids in foster care hear 'Your Mum's no good' all the time. Some kids are angry and so many people can't handle that. They feel 'I might as well go back on the gear'. The kid might have to talk about that anger. My daughter's had to be a parent at a very young age, even her Dad was an addict and she's had to drag him out of pubs and tell him to come home….I do counselling now, I've been there. I want to give something back. I think there should be more support for teenagers and more support for parents." *Jess was once in Holloway. One daughter now 16.*

"I have one son 16 years old and what a cock-up I've made of it all. I've been a heroin addict for twenty years. My son has seen it all. He is streetwise which isn't always a good thing. As a child he never did without material things, but even though I was there in body I wasn't there in as I should have been. He was starved of affection as the drugs were more important to me. I didn't realize at the time- I only thought of my need for drugs. That was the most important thing in my life. I wasn't there for him. I didn't take any interest in him. It is all a learning process. Being a parent isn't easy. My wife (his mother) died when he was 5. Looking back he has had an awful life through one thing and another.

I remarried but things didn't work out between my new wife and son. She took the brunt of a lot of his anger and I continued to take drugs. My son was expelled from school when he was 11 years old. That was a difficult time. We eventually found somewhere else that would have him. My son hates his step Mum. Nobody has taken any decisions for him really. Even though I've been in prison I've been involved as much as I can. When he was 14 years old I put him into voluntary care. He had been passed from one family member or friend to the other. He had lived everywhere. I was still using drugs. I thought that by putting him into care he would be fostered and have proper love and a home that I had been unable to give him. I wanted him to have a normal life, be settled, have friends and go to school. It didn't work out being in care - he didn't attend school, he started using soft drugs, he even turned more violent. He was then moved out of the area into another home. I had the chance of going to a rehab jail, but down in Devon miles from home and my son. Social services paid for him to visit me each month. That was great. Being in rehab helped me so much I could start to think and take stock of my life. I love my son very much. I just never understood the responsibility – nobody can show you. I wish I had listened to others, maybe I wouldn't have made the mistakes I have. I want to make it up to my son. My son enjoyed the home he was at – he started to go to school, he even had a part time job. I loved his visits. We both looked forward to them. We always had plenty to talk about. Unfortunately the home was out of his area and funding etc… all the red tape. The bigwigs decided he should move back to a home in our hometown. This was a bad move. He stayed back with his step-mum, but that didn't work out. Then he went to live with some old friends of mine. People never really tell you what's happening. When you are in jail they say what they think you should know. I think that's the worst thing about being a parent in jail. When you have problems you have no control over them. I've tried hard to keep control, well for me, it's control for the first time ever. Since I've been in prison. When you have problems you have no control over them.

I've tried hard to keep control, well for me, it's control for the first time ever. Since I've been in prison I've attended all kinds of meetings with social services and the education department. The staff here have helped me. Now I'm clean from drugs, I look at everything differently. It's like I'm starting my life again and I can actually see things going on around me. Whether it's on the out or I'm in here I am much more focused. I know what I want now..My son lost his Mum and Gran when he was five. I lost my wife and mother. I suppose we never came to terms with it. I got him bereavement counselling and drugs help, but he gave up on it. He thinks he can do it on his own. That frightens me as I know you can't. You need help from others. You have to listen and learn. I feel now with all the help I've had in prisons, I want to put the theory into practice. I want to be a proper parent for the first time. Looking back I've learned so much and now I want to show him he can trust me. I'm due out in five months if I get parole. He is just waiting for me to get out. I feel that is a pressure. My family all expect me to get parole – but what if I don't? I am optimistic about the future. I will try. If I can try while being in prison I can do it out there with help." *C. 35 years, HMP Kirklevington Grange his son is 16.*

"I have one daughter who will be 7 next birthday. Throughout her life I've only spent about 6 -7 weeks at home with her. I have been in and out of prison. It didn't help me at first. I went to a local prison and I knew most of the users there; I had nearly as much when I was inside as I did on the out. Then I decided if I was going to ever be clean and take my responsibilities seriously I needed to do something. When I was arrested I asked to be sent away from my local area so that I didn't have the contact with the old crowd. I knew it would be difficult for visiting but my girlfriend came every week with the baby. I think if you want to make a go of it you have to get rid of the shit from the past. I had to learn the hard way, and worse even harder for my girlfriend and daughter. I think of what I've put them through, and how I've wasted so much money on drugs. They could have had a better life. My girlfriend has been great. She lets me know what's going on. I don't bother with my old so-called mates. I want a clean break from that life." I don't know if I could have done things differently. I lived in a rough area and everyone was doing the same. It was hard to be different but I intend to now. I want to make up for the time I've had away from her.

My Dad left my Mum and me when I was 9. I think if he had been around I wouldn't have ended up like this, but my Mum loved me; she was probably too soft with me. Looking back now she was just trying to make up for my Dad not being there. I don't want to know him. For years I used to look at this man near where I lived and thought he was my Dad, but it wasn't. I'm not bothered about him and if I did see him I wouldn't speak." *P. HMP Kirklevington Grange, aged 27. Serving a five year sentence, awaiting parole after two years six months served. His daughter is now 7.*

"Owen has no excuse. Compared to a lot of young people, he had every chance of a successful life – DRUGS! the child you knew is no longer there and it's hard to get them back"

Lorna 54, her son is 28

"I didn't know how my family was going to survive, I was worried about my finances, how the mortgage was going to be paid, I get disability but that isn't enough, I was just so hysterical."

Elise, 35.

"We have got around the problem of him coming out; we are taking him to Blackpool because he has no contacts for drugs there. Accommodation is cheap there and it's a different location to get him as far away from here as possible. He will have community service to do but we've arranged that with the probation officer, we will have to fund him until he can get a job. He might be able to get some seasonal work and then get a reference for a proper job. We couldn't have him back here, it would be impossible, he has too many contacts for drugs. We were hoping that he'd get a longer sentence than he did to give us more time to sort things out, we are going through this sentence we are being punished for being innocent. I think Will is too in a way because being involved with drugs like this is a disease, I had no idea what being on drugs meant, the way it hurts everybody until it happened to us. My doctor knows that Will's a heroin addict, he said that I should throw Will out, I asked the doctor if he would throw his son out, Will is our boy and we don't want him to die. As long as we can help Will we will, we don't want him to die from heroin, it's so hard for him, he cant get into rehab, the doctor says that in this town alone there's more than two hundred addicts and there's no room in rehab for Will." *Mary, her son is 22.*

Booze, fags and pills.

"I smoke a lot, I can't at work but in the evenings I smoke an awful lot, I worry because I get a bad chest and the more I worry the more I smoke, it's a vicious circle The doctor tried to give me anti depressants but I wouldn't have them, our problems come from our son taking drugs and the doctor wanted to give me drugs to take. Sam and I we have only got ourselves to help one another through it." *Mary 48, her son Will is in prison for the second time.*

"I went to the doctor but was too embarrassed to tell him the truth of things. I told him that something terrible had happened in the family, I don't know what he must have thought had happened. I didn't take medication from him though; I was too frightened in case I wouldn't be able to come off it after the last time. I'd taken so many of those pills before that I came out in a rash and I looked like I had the measles. I have a strong faith in the church though and that helps me through. I took to the bottle once or twice but it's no good hiding away behind pills or drink, you have to face up to things sometime."
Sandra, had three sons in prison at the same time.

"I smoke, but not very much, I don't drink, I'm on anti depressants, I've been on them since before he went in there. It's hard for me because he's making me do the sentence with him." *Teresa 24, partner serving three years.*

"I don't smoke but I'm an alcoholic, It's under control and I did have a drink problem in the past but it's as they say, once an alcoholic always an alcoholic. I got so down one night that I drank a bottle of vodka and wrote and told Tommy – I've drank a bottle of vodka tonight." *Lucy 34, partner Tommy sentenced to five months.*

Practicalities

> "We had never argued about money until he went in there, I've managed, I'm a born survivor, I've been living on income support, sending Tommy £50 a week and running a car and keeping the house and kids going because it's the only way I could get to visits."
>
> *Lucy 34, she has five children.*

CHAPTER EIGHT - PRACTICALITIES

Money

"I don't go out much because its so hard financially, it only takes me half an hour to get there but I don't know what I would have done if he'd been further away. He knows that if he steps out of line again I won't be there for him. It costs me £50 - £60 every month just in petrol and making sure he has money. I just keep plodding on; it's an almighty struggle. I tried applying for housing benefit they first gave some to me then 'phoned me at work one day and said I'd been overpaid by £900, I burst into tears at work, thankfully I went to the CAB (Citizens Advice Bureau) and got it all sorted but I was worried all the time.

At the beginning there were lots of things that went on that I didn't tell him, I kept plodding on, then it all got in such a state and I burst out with everything. He said I should have been telling him and now I do, I tell him everything rather than my Mum and Dad to keep worrying them, I need his opinions, it makes it easier to cope, I talk it all through with him. If I give up my job I'd have housing benefit and everything handed to me on a plate, the nursery is expensive, but I don't want to do that, I want to keep working, that family tax credit thing has been a great help."
Jasmine, her child is 18 months old, partner in prison for 22 months due out soon.

"I'm in so much debt 'cos of him being in there. To be honest the kids love going to see him because it's like an adventure for them. (he's not their father) It's difficult though as they want to do things and see things as well when we go which costs money as they see it as a day out. To be honest I think they think that going to visit my partner is an inconvenience in their day out!! I have tried to make it a bit fun for them but it costs so much money. I have to see him to keep myself sane, but I just can't afford to see him at the moment. I'm back at work now and I've had loads of support - my boss has been really understanding. At the moment I'm just plodding on - I can't think about it too much. I don't have much support for me - I don't get on with his Mum; his family hasn't seen him at all since he's gone back in." *Angie 27.*

"I'm on maternity leave at the moment so I still get money that way, I've always worked, I do three visits a week at the moment though while he's on remand and that does cost a lot." *Christina 25, partner awaiting sentence – they have a three week old baby.*

"The worst part is financial, I spend twenty quid a week getting here and I'm running up credit card bills, no, I can't pay them, I expect they'll come on top sometime but I'll cross that bridge when I come to it." *Sonya, husband only one year into an 18 year sentence, they have two children aged 8 and 4 years.*

"I'm working but only part time and it's really hard for money but my Mam helps. Visits cost a lot all of the time. He wants what's best for him but I can't have what's best for me, he wont get moved to a gaol nearer home because he wouldn't have things as good and I do not want to keep visiting where he is now, it's too far and I'm drained." *Teresa 24, her partner was given a three year sentence.*

"I don't send him money or nothing. I leave that to his family. I've got my kids to think of and they come first. My friend with four kids gets her bloke trainers and everything. I wouldn't do that, no luxuries for him mate when I've got my kids to think of." *L 25, 2 children.*

Counting the cost for families

"Things will be different when he comes out, once I've paid his debts off, I shall be left with nothing. No, if he wants something he'll have to wait for it this time, I just can't do it anymore he'll have to pay for things himself, although I still love him to bits. My finances will be all right, I don't have debts like he does, he hasn't lost his house or his contents, so it should be plain sailing for him really. He was earning more money than me before he went to prison. I haven't worked in 2½ years, I only receive sick money but I have given him all my sick money before now to get him out of shit street! When I have sold my house and paid off his debts I will spend more time focusing on myself. I can start a new life, hopefully. My sister in law took me out for lunch yesterday, which was really nice; I was like - ooh isn't this posh!" *Jean 45, supporting her son 21.*

"I feel like the family shouldn't have to send money, or be in a position where they feel like they have to as the family have suffered enough. I think that it is asking too much. Me and my mother had to share the cost of buying all the stuff for him, which made me feel resentful, as we hadn't done anything. Me and my Mum used to bend over backwards for him, buying him endless bars of chocolates, drinks etc whilst we were in there. But then afterwards I'd feel really angry at him that we were bending over backward for him, when we were struggling for money on the outside. About halfway through the sentence we started to get on better with him 'cos I felt like I was back in control of things, of him, because I just could walk away from him if I felt it was all getting too much." *Kerrie 24, visiting her brother in prison.*

"It was hard at the beginning, losing friends, visiting him in prison but although it sounds ridiculous I'm very happy now. I manage with money and get to see him once a week, my new employers are letting me have Wednesday mornings off and I work late another day so I can do visits."

"I don't get out but that's not because of babysitters, it's down to money, I get £100 a week and it's costing me £40 to see him. I looked at a form for assisted visits but put it down again 'cos it looked like I couldn't claim 'cos I had no proof he was living with me before he went in there. I will get a form and fill it in. He gets no luxuries, basically I'm doing enough, I feel sorry for him being in there and everything, I send him no money either, I think' you've done this not me! My kids come first and I'm just waiting to see what happens at court, how long he gets." *Lena 25 has two children – she's waiting to hear what sentence her partner will get.*

But some manage better on their own...

"I don't work and had to go on Income Support because Paul was the breadwinner, to be quite honest I'm managing fine because we had no debt or anything and Paul has never been in a high paid job so I'm quite good with money – always been able to manage."
Jackie 37, mother of three children.

"I managed fine with money when he wasn't at home, I'm the one with the brain as far as money's concerned, I saved a fortune in fact because I'm really good with money and he hasn't got a clue about how to manage things with money. Because he wasn't there to spend it, I've saved for us all to go on holiday. I had a lot of problems when he went in there, he was claiming benefits for us from the council and when he was put away it all stopped and I had a right performance to sort it all out." *Laura 23, mother of two young sons.*

"I think that support groups are badly advertised but they are so important- SHARP has been a real help, I just don't know what I would have done without them."

"I was OK for money because I work and my Mam looked after the kids but if it had been for any longer I don't know what I would have done." *Elaine 28, husband served six months, she has three children.*

"I work and have been fine financially, I've still had my husband's pay for the moment so things haven't been so bad."
Jane 38, husband was remanded in custody, they have two children.

"Adam and Sarah write letters to Paula and we take them to visit when we can but it's very hard on the money, we get no help."
Geraldine, grandmother looking after her daughters two children while she serves a ten year sentence.

Not qualifying for assistance

"It's taken me four hours on the train to get here and cost me £60, I only get £65 a week to live on, I can't get money for visits because we didn't live together properly before he came in, he was still supposed to be living at his Dad's place."
Dawn 22, visiting her boyfriend – she is three months pregnant.

The struggle to do it all

"I don't have time to think with the baby, working and decorating and going to see John, the people at work have been great, I need to take a half day holiday every week so that I can go and see him, I was up front and told them what was happening and they've been good about it all. If I go to see John at weekends you see, they (the prison) make you use up two VO's ,so you only get one visit a month and it's better to go every two weeks, better for May as well, that's all wrong I think." *Jasmine 23, 1 daughter 22 months.*

"He's been in and out for 11 years and nobody has really asked me how I cope. It's him or the kids or the family. It's like the olden days when women had to cope and just get on with it. I wish someone could have listened, but then I don't know what I would have said to them. I feel I've just rambled on to you, but it has made some sense to me." *JT. Husband in HMP Durham.*

Coping somehow

Mother

"You weaken sometimes because it gets to you, how many chances can you give someone? I work full time and that's the only thing that keeps me sane, that and having Sam, we are very close and talk about everything, we share the burden between us. I couldn't go to work the other Wednesday, I cracked up, my head hurt so much and Sam and I we talked and talked, I just kept thinking that I can't keep going through this. My boss doesn't know about anything, Sam 'phoned and told him that my car had broken down and I couldn't get to work. You sometimes want to curl up and die but you have to stay strong." *Mary, mother of Will 22.*

Wives and mothers

"I've had no help from the doctor, I didn't sleep for weeks and weeks – pacing the floor all night, sleeping tablets wouldn't have solved the problem plus my job is very demanding. Also, I didn't want to put my hands up to there being a problem. The minute I step out of the house I paint on my 'I'm coping' smile, then I put my mumsy head on for the kids, I have no other way of dealing with things I took my husband for granted as far as day to day things went, I'd get home from work and the girls would have done their homework and the dinner would be cooked – you don't know what you've got until you've lost it." *Jane 38, supporting her husband in prison and caring for their two daughters aged 8 and 6 years.*

"I think that my daughter needs counselling as she's taken it so hard, but she won't go. My partner's very ill. I feel like jumping off a roof sometimes but I'm quite strong."

Jill 47, supporting her son through his prison sentence.

"I can't fault the visitors centre at Durham, the woman there was great, I don't know if I'd have ever made it up there to see John without her because I felt physically sick, I might have backed out if it hadn't been for her and he (John) was worried if everything was going to be alright because he knows how I feel about all of that kind of thing."

"I've not been to see the doctor because of this, I've got on with it, and I'm a strong person, having kids helps you to keep going, if they see you cracking up they might follow, I've tried to keep things as normal as possible – it's like a death, you have to cope. I don't have much of a social life – not with a 7 month old, but I was never really one for going out anyway, always been a bit of a home bird, I have some good friends though and they all have kids so we have days out together and sometimes they come round and we'll have a take away and a bottle of wine. The hardest bit was leaving him at the end of visits, I'd come out blubbering, they are not nice places to leave someone and I was devastated but then I realized that I was only upsetting him, it's still hard but I'm more in control of myself now."
*Jackie 37, her husband was sentenced to 3*1/2 *years, they have three children.*

Mother
"I've survived, just, its not been easy but I've toughened. There was no experience of this in my family and having just lost my husband it was indescribable. I've met someone else now who shares my life – I would have killed myself. My new partner is very supportive of me and Owen, he has spent most of today moving Owen's things over to his new house, I'm very lucky."
Lorna 54, supporting her son Owen 28.

Husband and father
"You do learn to adjust to the situation, not that it's easy mind you! It has been a complete turn around in my life. What has happened has made us a stronger family I think. I've just tried to take things day to day otherwise you could become overwhelmed by what's going on." *Stuart 32, taking care of his three children and supporting his wife through her prison sentence.*

Who supports the supporters?
"I had the support of a group in Merseyside who were brilliant. I always hung onto the morals and values of our family and felt that he (M) would come out good because of that." *Mother of 24 year old son, ex- heroin addict now released.*

"I hid it all from my family. I got my support from his family really. I hid it from the children. I told the children he was working away."
Sue 36, two children aged 17 and 14.

"It's been difficult for me some of my mates know about my Dad. I don't talk to my Mum about it, but I don't want to. I talk to my best mate about it."
Nathan 11.

"We went to a support group for help but they were no good (Libra), they told us before he was locked up to throw him out but we couldn't do that to our own son. Now we think that his only chance is to get him out of the area. We can't keep going through this, he's an adult and we can't give him any more chances, he has to start taking things on board."
Mary 48, mother of Will 22.

"I have nobody to turn to with my problems, I tell the odd friend some things. How long are you supposed to be responsible for your kids? I hope the stint in prison teaches them both a lesson."
Sandra mother of 25 year old son.

"I'd be in pieces if I didn't have Mum and Dad, I'd sit in all day and be very lonely. He's been in before, this isn't the first time but what can you do? I have lots of support from my family, they are there for me and they help me financially and in lots of other ways, I've got plenty of help at home." *Christina 25, partner is remanded in custody. Their baby is three weeks old.*

"I tell my family bits of things but not everything, I was brought up to keep my problems to myself, I would never use a support group." *Sonya, husband serving 18 years.*

"I think that support groups are badly advertised but they are so important-SHARP has been a real help, I just don't know what I would have done without them."

"The social services came straight round to see what was going to happen with the kids but they soon cleared off when they knew we would keep them, they didn't want to know about any help we might need, we haven't seen them since except we asked for a new bed because they were having to share a bed and Adam was wetting it sometimes, the cheeky sods brought us a plastic mattress cover and that was the last we saw of them. There are three men's prisons on the Isle of Wight and there are people for prisoner's wives to go to but there's nothing there for kids and people with mothers or daughters inside, not that we've been able to find that is, so there's nothing and nobody for us. You try to talk to people about your problems but they don't want to know because they're only there for men prisoners, in London I think it's different."
Geraldine, grandmother of Adam and Sarah.

"I think the hardest thing has been trying to accept that my son would do that and that it isn't my fault. That was tough to try and stop blaming myself. But you can't go back, you can only go forward. SHARP really helped through that, to come to this point."

Alison 41.

"Sometimes I wish there was someone else to turn to and tell them just how I feel and how I cope or don't cope. Money is tight: we now can't pay the electric so it's on a meter which is a bloody pain."

"I don't mix with friends or anything, I tend just to do my own thing, I don't need to be around people, I try to keep myself busy – I'm a mad cleaner in the house. I've never been to or even thought about contacting a support group; I wouldn't want to do that' *Teresa 24, partner John is serving a three year sentence.*

"I've not got a huge amount of friends, I'm more the sort to keep things to myself. I have two friends who I'd sit for hours with, just talking, one of them is going through a bad time with a divorce and I would try to concentrate on her problems, it helps to do that – think of someone else's problems not your own *Jane 38, mother of two girls, her partner was remanded in custody.*

"At home, only my friend and one of his friends knew that he had gone inside, I didn't tell anybody." *Elaine 28, husband served 6 months imprisonment, mother of three children.*

"The social services are involved with the kids now and it's so unnecessary because if there had been help and support for us in the beginning, nothing would have gone so far." *Lucy 34, coping with five children while partner Tommy served five months.*

"It's hard, very hard visiting him but Shirley at the visitors centre has been very helpful." *Mary, visiting her 22 year old son.*

"When I got there for the first visit the women at the visitors centre were really helpful, they explained everything to me and it wasn't so bad then." *Laura 23, visiting her husband for the first time.*

"Many people are aware of the situation - the only help I got was from a neighbour. My wife's family doesn't want to know - they aren't at all interested now - we used to see them quite a bit before this happened - I have had no help from them. I also have to look after my wife's father who lives with us, so at least the children get to see one of their grandparents." *Stuart 32, visits his wife in prison.*

"None of my family live close but they were all very supportive, also our business customers were supportive and stood by us which was a help, nobody could believe that my husband would rob his own house, there was absolutely no need for it, it was a real shock for everyone when they found out he had been sent to prison." *Elise 35.*

"I did have lots of support around me; the people at work were really understanding of all the problems I was having, of the depression. Although I felt bad 'cos everyone on my Dad's side were sniggering behind our backs." *Kerrie 24, her brother served a prison sentence.*

"My step Dad has been very supportive of us, he was a Samaritan and trained Samaritans in prisons and he writes to Tony every week. I don't have many mates from before but the people I work with now all know the truth about where Tony is and I have a good social life, going out with them. Tony likes me to have a life and get out and do things. I went on a walk last week and took 'photo's of the whole walk and sent them in to him. We are doing a sponsored walk for ADFAM together in a couple of weeks because they have helped us so much and they are so poor. Tony will be walking around the prison yard for three days and I'll be doing it at the same time. The people at work have been great, I have new friends now and the old ones can please themselves. My mother won't support me at all but that's her choice I suppose."
Gina 31, partner Tony is serving a life sentence.

"I'm twenty and my partner is nineteen. The baby was planned, she's nine months. I'd been on a training course. She'd been pregnant at 16 and decided not to have it. We both dreaded abortion. It was a hard decision I left school. My Mum supports her and me in every way. That's the only family support. Her Dad is there but I've never had a conversation with him - he is really stubborn. My Mum and Dad are supportive, Dad's a workaholic he works abroad a lot only in the last twelve months. I have one brother and sister and Gran lived across the road – very extended family. A good childhood."
J. 20, Feltham.

Disciplining the children

For most parents there are arguments to be had over disciplining children. Perhaps one is too soft, one too strict. Or one wants to be loved because he (and it is usually he) sees so little of them, while Mum is there most of the time and finds herself endlessly correcting the kids. Parents also want to be backed up by their partner and feel let down when this does not happen. Add the prison ingredient to these universal problems and there are new aspects to this dilemma. In the comments shown here we see views from all sides.

"Kids ask their Daddies to come play in the play area but we are not allowed to move from our seat, so our kids think that we don't want to go and have fun with them or that we're not interested (how wrong). I would do anything to get the chance to run around mad with my daughter."

Fathers

"I find it difficult to discipline them while I'm in here, but I know I need to. My wife says I have to tell them off, so they know I'm still involved. I know they'll play her up. Kids do that in normal circumstances, so it must be worse with a Dad in prison. When I 'phone my wife she always tells them 'Dad can hear you shouting or being naughty."
D. 28 HMP Holme House, sentence 4 years served 2 years. Parole date set. 3 children, 2 girls aged 8 and 4 and a boy aged 2 years.

"I couldn't discipline, how can I – what position am I in to do that? I can't preach what I don't practice. I talk about their attitude sometimes as they squabble between themselves. Typical sisters."
R. 42 HMP Loudham Grange sentence 9 years two teenagers.

"I couldn't tell my daughter off. I think that bothers my girlfriend, but on an hour visit or a weekly visit home I don't want to spoil it. But even before I came in I didn't use as much discipline as her Mam. Probably it's good we are both different, but we are lucky we can discuss it. I think it's a good idea for the men or women to do courses about looking after kids – it's not easy."
P. 24 HMP Kirklevington Grange his daughter is now aged four. She was two when he went to prison on a four year sentence. Awaiting decision on parole.

> "I learned that my son is not a possession. He is not there to be owned and ordered about to do as he is told, but to be loved, cherished, cared for and to be fed the right information in order to grow strong."
>
> *R. 26 On remand Gateside Prison.*

"I can't give my daughter discipline. My girlfriend and I talk about it but I can't spoil the short time I have with her." *P. HMP Kirklevington Grange aged 27 daughter of 7, served two years 6 moths of a five year sentence, awaiting parole.*

Mothers

"I try to tell him what is going on in our lives. I don't hide things from him. What's the point? If the kids are playing up I tell them I will tell their Dad. The youngest one says 'What can he do where he is?' So it is difficult. But when they visit he tells them what is what. I find it difficult with my eldest son. He is at an age when he will be experiencing sex with young girls. What can I say or his Dad say to him? What advice can we give? Tell him to be careful. I get mad at my husband sometimes and tell him he should be the one telling his sons how to go on."
Mother of two teenage sons, husband in prison on a seven year sentence. Acklington.

A teenager's view:

"He asks us questions about why we are being naughty and that, but when he comes back we are going to ask him the same thing." *K. 16*

Parenting Courses

"The parenting course here has made me realize and think about so many things I know I didn't appreciate about the pregnancy and baby stages, but I want to make up for it now. I think I can develop as long as I keep letting him know I love him. When he's a bit older I'll start to write little letters. I must learn not to be resentful of others that have time with him now. I'm pleased I've done the course, but I can't wait for the time when we are together. It's true when people say crime doesn't pay. It really doesn't when you see the pain you put them through and how much you miss out with your children. I'll try to explain to his Mum that I would like some time with him and do things together. I don't want to be one of those MacDonald's Dads, that only sees their kids for a couple of hours. I want to be there for the homework the fun and the hard times.

I'm doing lots of courses in here to help me when I get out, so that my son can see that I can help him. I get butterflies before I 'phone or see him. I don't know why, but I do. I get really excited when I know he's coming to visit. I've made a big mistake but I don't want my son to suffer any more because of me. I don't want this life for him. I hope I can teach him how to get on in life and not by the mess I've made of things."

C 27, HMP Wolds child is now 3 sentence is 12 years.

"I am 22 years old and I am currently a guest at her majesty's pleasure. I have been in this vicious cycle for years now and I can't seem to break away from it. I started off from 15 years of age and when I was 16 my girlfriend feel pregnant. She had a wee girl and we called her Chrissie. She was in and out of hospital with problems from birth but I was never around as I was always in and out of prison, which I am gutted about - because my daughter is four now and at nursery. I

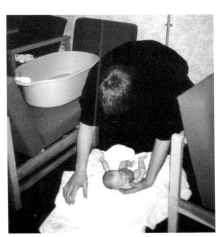

haven't seen any of her birthdays or Christmases. I feel a failure of a father sometimes and I miss my daughter very very much. Whoever is reading this will ask themselves: if he loves and misses his daughter so much then what is he doing in and out of prison? I am not proud of what I did but I will tell you if I haven't got a job then I will do what it takes…It is hard having kids and being in prison, as kids ask their Daddies to come play in the play area but we are not allowed to move from our seat, so our kids think that we don't want to go and have fun with them or that we're not interested. (How wrong). I would do anything

> "I've done the parenting course here. I know we can't hide or should not hide things from our children. It taught me to look at this point of view. If more people knew about being a parent, society might be better."
>
> *J. 43, HMP Wolds sentence: ten years. Youngest child is 11 two older children not in UK ages 14 and 13.*

"I've tried since I've come in here to do all the courses and I want to be a Listener. It's my way of giving back, for getting a chance to improve myself and hopefully to help others. I've got to look forward, I would go mad if I thought about the past all the time. I'm lucky I have a purpose."

D. 28, HMP Holme House sentence 4 years served two, D has a wife and three children.

to get the chance to run around mad with my daughter - do face painting drawings colouring etc. Once I heard about the Parenting Course I was very interested. I never did it to try and be a better Dad, as I am a great Dad to Chrissie and everyone does things different. I did the course to get a stronger bond with her. As part of the group we were to get a once in a lifetime chance to have a two hour visit - get to run around, do face painting, read books, watch a video and so much more. Also apart from having the chance to spend two great hours with my daughter, there were certain things about the classroom work that I found interesting . I personally thought the Parenting Group was an eye opening experience. I enjoyed it very much. We learned what our loved ones go through while we are away from home and how they cope. Then we went on to ask about what we tell our kids about being in prison? Do we tell lies or tell the truth? We also got briefed on help and advice available to our families. So I also benefited from that. The one thing I picked up was what to say on the 'phone and in letters to our kids. We then got that visit that we were all looking forward to, family and us. I couldn't believe that I was actually getting the chance to have fun with Chrissie. It was brilliant. We never had a better visit than that one. I had a great two hours. We got photos taken, we were on video. Chrissie had a great time then we learned how to maybe save a life, both adults and children. I found that beneficial. We got the chance to make videos for our kids. It was bedtime stories, we read our kids' favourite books and we put it on video and sent them out so next time one of my daughter's friends says she hasn't got a Dad, she can show them the video of me telling stories. I really did enjoy the group and I hope other guys get the chance to do the same as I would definitely recommend it. There was one bad point after having had that two hour visit and that was having to tell Chrissie that I can't move out of my seat the next time I see her."
G. 22, HMP Greenock prison. Scotland.

"It was a really good visit. Chrissie really enjoyed running about with her Dad instead of playing herself. I think it's great for the fathers to get involved."
Chrissy's Mum.

"When I was asked if I'd like to go on the parenting course I basically took the opportunity on the grounds that it was going to get me out of my cell a little more. Just as important it was going to get me a two hour visit with my daughter Stevie. But little did I know how much this class was going to teach me and how much I was going to be looking forward to each session. After a couple sessions I began to realise that I wasn't alone in my way of thinking. I started to understand that every guy on this course had the same genuine concerns that had caused me many a restless night. I began to hear how these guys felt, how they coped and started to use this to my advantage.

One particular session on the course sticks in my mind more than the others and this was the day we discussed the effects of how our imprisonment affected our partners, families and most important to me, our kids. It helped me realise that although I was locked up in here they were also being punished for my crimes. This thought hit home as they say! Beforehand I thought that as long as I acted a good father then that was okay, but I realised quite quickly that being a good father wasn't about acting it was about doing. Well what do I think I've learned from this course? I think I've learned that being a parent is about hundreds of different things. Beforehand I thought that as long as I acted as a father then that was OK. But I realised rather quickly that being a good father wasn't about acting it it was about doing. It was putting all the things I'd heard and learned on the course into action and I could honestly see the benefits in my relationship with my daughter as quickly as my first visit with her. It also made me write to her more and when writing I found it a lot easier. I'd always found it hard to write to a four year old and now here I was actually enjoying it. All I can say to anyone who's a father in prison, if you have the opportunity to take part in a parenting course, what have you got to lose? In my opinion you can only gain and more importantly your gain is your children's gain." *S. HMP Greenock.*

"Because I'm doing the Family Learning programme I get to see the children more often, twice a week, which is great. Mondays are family days. It's the highlight of my week. My little lad comes in, which is great. He can get to know me and me him. The oldest girl only comes once every three weeks (on Mondays) as we don't want to upset her schoolwork. She's doing so well. The middle girl comes before or after nursery and I get time with their Mam on her own. I feel the programme is really good for me and my family. I married when

I was young, we wanted kids and were delighted when they were born. It's not unusual around our way to get married and have kids young. I wouldn't change having kids young. I hope I can be a better Dad. I think I am a better Dad now, being a drug user isn't good, so things must be better. Having a family can be a pressure as you have someone else to think about. You don't want to fail them or yourself."
D. 28, 3 children 8, 4 and 2 years.

"On remand it's just like the kennels: feed them, take them for a little walk and then bang them up again."

"The video has given her great comfort and enjoyment. She watches the tape constantly day and night and she even talks back to her Dad. All the family watch the video and we feel we have a part of Richard back home with us. I think it's a great idea and I'm pleasantly surprised it has happened in prison. It is a credit to the Prison office's understanding of how much children miss and are affected by their father's absence." *Mary. Husband in HMP Greenock.*

Can prison make a difference?

"Lots of things in my life are starting to come together now. Prison was needed in my life. Things would have got worse. I don't know how things would have ended up but it wouldn't have been good. I have a much better relationship with my parents and sister. This prison tries to keep everyone together as a family. When my family visits and we all sit around together talking, it brings us closer together, more than we have been in years. When I do get out of prison I'll have to start all over again in a lot of ways, but by doing the courses here, it helps you think about the things you can change or want to change." *G. 37, HMP Wolds. 10 year sentence, three children, divorced from wife, but still in contact over children.*

"I think doing the parenting course helped me more than anything. I actually feel things are better now between me and my girlfriend. I am able to look at how things are for her at home. I know the kids play her up. I can tell as soon as I see them on visits, just by looking at their faces."
J. 24, HMP Wolds, daughters 6 and 4. Sentence: 4 years.

"I'm doing a degree course in here and I've done all the courses available. I hope my girls can learn from this…that I'm really trying hard."
R. 42, father of two teenagers, Loudham Grange sentence 9 years.

"When I was in Durham, I put in lots of applications for lots of things but never heard nothing. I'm still waiting for my asthma inhalers. For the length of time I was in, there was nowt to do – just books (J can't read) it was doing me head in – no air and moving me all the time. Locked up 23 hours a day. But the worst was the asthma. When I got to Wealstun it was brilliant. I got my asthma inhalers the next day. I went straight into education – they started teaching me to read and I picked mushrooms. I definitely enjoyed it. I learned how to put a computer on, I learned something – even in three weeks. Wealstun was great. At first I was frightened, you go first in closed then they move you to an open wing. There is one officer and you can walk around freely. I saw the fence and I could've gone over, but I wouldn't have gone over the fence. They said they gonna try and get me a job." *J.32, now released.*

"I don't feel any stigma to being in prison. It's helped me. I've learnt about myself, I've done lots of courses and I work. The staff help me. I've learned to appreciate what I've got in all ways. I feel prisoners should chill and make the most of the time in jail. I think if you can start to be honest with yourself it will be easier to be honest with others and a better parent or partner."
P. HMP Kirklevington Grange.

"I think him going to prison has done him the world of good, he's told me that he can get drugs in prison really easily but he's not doing them. I mean he is a different man, he really is. I don't understand the levels in prison but I know that he has got to a good level now. If he can pass the next drug test then he will be upgraded again to a CAT D."
Jean 45, supporting her son 21 in prison.

"He thinks and I think, that if more people got life sentences they would get more out of the prison system and have less chance of getting into more trouble, it's the best thing that could have happened for him, it really is, it's the saving of him. When you're released gradually like that, you can do things right."
Gina 31, her partner has been offending since he was fourteen years old, he is now 34 and serving a life sentence.

"I do Education – computers. I've never been able to work one apart from the on/off switch – now I can actually use this time in prison. Prison is showing me I'm a person. I have needs too being a single parent with five children and five foster children for the last twenty three years, never been able to do anything for me. I have just finished a CSLA course and passed. I go to Gym four times a week, I have my hair permed, my nails have grown and I got them designed for my first visit for my daughter who is in second year Law because of me. I have even put on weight and do drama, creative writing with Tanika Gupta who does scripts for Crossroads, Eastenders. I know I did wrong and I must pay for my crime, which I am doing, but I'm also gaining confidence and learning how to think and enhance my future. I got eighteen months and should get tagging. I pray, go to church and sit with other inmates and think in my own space and wonder how I would have achieved all this education on road - being a Mum, shopping, cooking, washing, housework, gardening, nurse, friend…the list was endless. All I need now and am praying for is my inter-prison visit to see my husband as we are co-defendants. I miss him so much it hurts, but we're learning a lot more respect for each other and learning new things about out qualities and worths - more than just looking after your family. I've contacted the children's father now it's his turn to care for his children no matter if he has a new family. My children come first so now he can have the responsibility as I am worrying enough about them.

So just to let you know that I've learned a lesson both ways – paying for my crime and getting myself an education and building my confidence as a unique individual. Thank you for this opportunity to let people know what it's like."
J. age not given, mother of five and five foster children. HMP Winchester – she sent this written contribution.

"Mr Mac is the only one who is safe yeah, 'cos he kinda puts he self out, sets goals for me tells me where I'm going wrong and where I'm doing right."
C. 15, Feltham YOI.

"It will be hard for my girlfriend to suddenly have someone else around, we might argue about who gets to look after our daughter. She wants me home, but I think she likes looking after herself. She's a chef and the grandparents all help."

D. age 20, HMP YOI Brinsford, daughter aged three.

Making the best of things or denial?

"He's a very very intelligent lad my son, too clever, he did a really big series of frauds, victimless crimes though. His boss where he used to work thought very very highly of him, gave him a brilliant reference for court, keeping a job there for him for when he gets out. He's doing an open university degree in here, loves education, he's OK here, gets on well with all the other lads, gets on well with the staff and everything, he's been trained by the Samaritans while he's been here, he's always at the gym, keeps himself fit, he looks really well, fit and that. I just let it all go over my head, his Mum here (Sandra) worries more, I drive her here once a month, and to see the other lad but that's closer. He's alright here, he'll just keep his head down 'till he's out, he's got a great sense of humour… from Liverpool isn't he?"
Dave has two sons in prison, one was due out in April 2002, and the other is three years into a 6$\frac{1}{2}$ year sentence.

He got worse in prison.

"My son was 15 years and 3 months when he was sent down. But he wasn't beaten up because he knew the other lads in there from the estate and they sort of took him under their wing like. They left him alone at 15, they were older and wiser. But he got in with them then and they're his big mates. It's not that he fell in with a bad crowd – he is the bad crowd. At 15 he was in for 15 months in a YOI in Rugby. Glen Parva then Onley.

My son moved on inside and he's now on remand for dealing at 21. He's had very little education inside and never had a job. He's been in 15 months and 18 months with constant moves. Now he's on his 4th move since March (July now). No courses are possible if you're moved, but on remand he wouldn't get them anyway. He's been in Leicester, Liverpool and Manchester. If he'd had a good probation officer it could have been different. He went on a driving course once. He'd been on a motorbike with a friend driving and there was this accident his friend died on the motorbike and my son was very badly injured. On remand it's just like the kennels: feed them, take them for a little walk and then bang them up again. At least before, when he was convicted, he got into the gym and built up these impressive muscles, but you don't go to the gym on remand. It accumulates you see, he's serving a sentence and then as one is finished other things comes up from the past. He's got a sentence, conditional bail and unconditional bail all at once. There are lots of cases. At least he doesn't have a child." *Jeannie.*

"It has done him the world of good - he now hasn't done drugs for 2 years. Before that he didn't even understand what we said to him to try and help him. I didn't like Glen Parva, Lichfield is much better, the Officers are much nicer - more relaxed and they talk to the lads nicely. I think that they just have a more forward way of thinking. They really seem to believe in rehabilitation, my son works out in the gardens now, which he is really getting on well with. I was so pleased the prison actually made an effort and thought about what he could do that was suitable for him and what he could progress in." *Alison 41.*

"This may sound mad but coming into prison was the best thing that happened to me. I probably would have been dead if I didn't get this sentence. I only thought of myself and drugs. It was my life. I feel I was never there for my family. How my wife stood by me I don't know. She's educated and has much more about her. I'm not or was not a nice person. The life I was leading was wrong, not just for me but for them. I was a bad father and partner. Because I'm doing the Family Learning Programme I get to see the children more often, twice a week which is great. I suppose we are lucky as we live locally so visits are not bad to get to." *D. 28, HMP Holme House sentence 4 1/2 years served 2. three children, two girls 8 and 4 and boy of 2.*

"It was too short, if he'd been sentenced to two years and served a year it would have given him the fright he needed, as it was, it just made him harder. They had given him strong anti depressants; it took months to get them out of him so how was the system going to benefit him, what was the point? He was barely conscious through the sentence so there was no chance of rehabilitation." *Lorna 54, her son 22 has a drug problem.*

"Shaun should be home in November, they've agreed to him having HDC, I think it'll be hard for him when he first comes home, I expect he'll be overwhelmed with everything and everyone."

Christina 25, she and Shaun have a three week old baby.

Can you keep your job?

"I don't work now, it got too much with the kids and all."
Geraldine, taking care of her grandchildren while their mother serves a ten year sentence.

"I live with my Mum and Dad, they're brilliant, I couldn't cope without them, they help me financially and with Claire. I tried to keep working full time at first, I did it for four months but then I couldn't manage it, I realised it was too much for me. I still work weekends." *Christina 25, her partner is awaiting sentence, their baby was born three weeks ago.*

"Before this happened I was working full time and now I'm a full time househusband! But it's surprising how quickly you adjust- I have to look after the house, 3 kids and a father in law, it made me learn about the things that I had taken for granted before." *Stuart 32, his wife is serving a prison sentence.*

"When he first went to prison we just existed - nothing more- my husband stopped work 'cos he just couldn't cope- before my son went to prison my husband was very ambitious in his career and he just lost his will. I felt like I wanted to solve the problem, the only problem was though; I didn't know what it was."
Alison 41.

Getting Out
and Life Beyond

CHAPTER NINE - GETTING OUT AND LIFE BEYOND

So many different feelings all at once...

"I have mixed feelings about Paul coming home, scared, nervous, happy – all thrown into one, it's different feelings at different times. I'll have to get used to him being home again, it's just as hard for them – we've got to learn to get to know each other again – we'll have to start again." *Jackie 37, husband received a first prison sentence of 3.1/2 years, they have three children.*

"I used to travel to Devon although it's such a long way, the work they do there with drug users is much better than locally so I encouraged him to go there knowing he would be much better off than in Walton or Manchester. Inside I was blaming my son, it was his fault, I was angry with him, but he was in prison so I couldn't let him know that. I worried more about him coming home, it's rotten having a son in jail and it might sound like a rotten thing to say but when he was in there I knew where he was, I worried all the time about him coming out and getting back in with his mates, because then you don't know what's going off." *Claire, Mother of 22 year old.*

"My family will support me when I leave and whatever I need to get back on my feet and love – friends are difficult to break free from – not all of them – three friends are in here. I trust them, but my friends on the road are snakes. There will be people looking to kill me, to do with my crime, you see what I'm saying. I haven't been able to talk to my family. I don't want them to get involved." *B. 17, Feltham YOI Remand, third time in jail.*

"She's had to learn to cope on her own, and she's got good at it – maybe she takes pride in it. And then you come, expecting everything to be like it was. You're not the master of the house any more."

"Going back home is strange and it does cause big conflict all round for everyone. It's something that's taken for granted, you automatically think you'll fit in and your family will accept you. But in reality there are a lot of unsaid issues that cause the conflict. When I got out last time it was difficult to fit back into the home routine. It was strange being back in with the family. There is a pressure on us to fit back in and I did find it hard. I suppose they must have, but it's not something we talked about. Maybe we should have. I can't change things now." *R.42, sentence 9 years served 3. Loudham Grange two daughters aged 14 and 16 recently divorced after 21 years.*

"When they're in, you know where they are. It's a sort of relief really. But there are other tensions, like the build up to the visit. There is so much to say but nothing to talk about. It unearths emotions in you deep within. But I couldn't tell him how I felt. He knows, we are close. I used to think I couldn't bear it if he didn't live at home. But now perhaps I'd feel relieved if he said he was going to live in another country. But then how would I manage to visit him?" *Jeannie who visits her son, 21, who has served two sentences and is facing more.*

"I think when he comes out it will be difficult to get the trust back, I'll probably keep asking myself 'is it all going to happen again?' But I certainly don't want to let my son know that I have doubts otherwise he will feel guilty forever and that isn't fair and he has paid for what he has done. We are going to try and work on it together as a family - it won't be easy for instance if something goes missing in the house - he'll think that we think he has stolen it and vice versa. I have found that 'footprints in the sand' prayer very helpful to get me though this, my faith is quite important to me." *Alison 41.*

"When he comes home he tries ordering me about at first like 'Get me a drink'. I say 'Where've you left your manners?' he is demanding and looking down his nose at us. It is a front he has to put on in there and takes time for it to return to normal. It's like walking on eggshells at first but it wears off."
Jeannie, her son is 15 and has served two sentences, one of fifteen months and one of eighteen months.

"It's been hell basically. I actually met him whilst he was in prison and I was visiting a friend but then we split up, as the pressure was too much. On the day he was released he was gate arrested and got another 10 years. I just couldn't believe it, I thought I could just about cope with the first sentence but then when he got another ten years I just couldn't work out how I was going to get through it, it just feels like it's never going to end. I think he is destined to spend his life going in and out of prison." *Angie 27.*

"You've got to be realistic. I know I'll have to readjust when I get home. I hope to go to an open prison and then it can be gradual – I don't know what will be best. It would be difficult for my wife, she has her own way… and in a strange way I have my routine here. It will take time for all of us. My youngest girls says I've got to sleep on the sofa when I come home as she and her brother sleep with their Mam. We've decided we'll redecorate their bedroom to get them back into it. I've got to be realistic - things will be difficult for everyone. I want my kids to enjoy a normal life whatever that is – I don't want them using drugs like I did. I've stopped all contact with others I knew who use drugs. I would even move areas if we needed to. If I didn't change I would have lost everything." *D. 28, HMP Holme House served 2 years of a four and a half year sentence.*

"I think he'll be OK when he gets out, he's coming to live with us, everybody's got expectations about him coming home and he does worry about this. He'll be on HDC for a couple of months so he'll stay with us then but I think Patrick will soon want his own place to live because he's very independent. I think we'd rather have him home, at least we'd know things, If there was another problem I hope he'd turn to us." *Louise supporting son (24) serving a three year sentence.*

"He thinks he'll be the boss when he comes out, but I've been on my own. It will be really strange. We didn't live together before. I don't know how it will all work out. We will first have to try."

S. she is 18 years old now, the baby is 7 months. Partner aged 21, is in HMP Durham.

143

"I think when he comes out it will be difficult to get the trust back, I'll probably keep asking myself, 'is it all going to happen again?' But I certainly don't want to let my son know that I have doubts otherwise he will feel guilty forever and that isn't fair and he has paid for what he has done."

"When I think about how my girlfriend used to travel all the way to see me, and with a baby. Then when she was a toddler. That can't have been easy for both of them. It does make you feel guilty and I wonder how I'll fit back in full time - we'll just have to take it slowly. Other people say 'just get on with it' or 'take it easy'. But I think everyone is different, and that's all you can do. It must be more difficult for my girlfriend; she has the worry of it all; me coming home; how things will be. Will I keep clean? There is so much going on but through this you can't forget there is a child; and I won't this time."
P. HMP Kirklevington Grange, age 27, daughter aged 7. sentence 5 years, served 2 years 6 months, awaiting parole.

"When we put him straight on the tagging thing, told him that we didn't want him home, his eyes filled up with tears and his lip was quivering but I've had to tell him how I feel these last couple of months, how much this has affected us. I told him that we needed more time to sort things out and that 'Mum has your clothes to wash and iron' Maybe he did think about things after that a little bit because he sent his Dad a letter saying 'don't worry Dad, I know that you and Mum need more time to sort things out,' letters sometimes express things better and Will is in a cell on his own so he has a lot of time to think things over."
Mary 48, visiting her son Will 22.

"What happens when he comes out is at the back of my mind, I try not to think about it too much but it's always there. I hope he's not going to be so stupid again. Every time I see him or get a letter from him he always says that he is so so sorry and that he never wants to go back to prison, I'm sorry what for he's done." *Jean 45, supporting her son 21.*

"I've stopped decorating now, I'm saving that last bit for when he gets home, and the garden, it'll be the summer then and he can do that as well." *Jasmine 23, visiting partner serving 18 months.*

"I thought that once we'd got it over, it would go easier, but actually it was easier when he was in Prison than now he's out 'cos his mother knew where he was, she said she knew he was safe when he was in prison. Myself, like for the crime he did, I know it's a terrible thing to say but I'm glad he was caught like, he did time and I hope this has put him on the right track." *Ken 65, his son served a prison sentence.*

Will he fit back into my life?

"I don't know where he'll fit back into my life, I would want things to be different than they were before, he's done an anger management course but his real problem is with the jealousy, I just hope he sorts his head out while he's in there."
Teresa 24, her partner is serving three years.

"I know its very hard for some people but for me personally, I feel like its not happening to me, you know, like its all happening to someone else, I just get on with it and don't think about things. I was five months pregnant when he went away and I had to go through it all on my own, the labour and everything with just my seven-year-old little boy. His Mum is really good though and I've got some good mates. Basically I'm enjoying motherhood with no man stressing me out, I'm my own boss and aint got no one telling me do it like this or like that."
Lena 25, mother two boys aged 7 years and six months, her partner is remanded in custody.

"If Tommy had been shown on a peak chart it would have been pointed right down when he first went in, then lots of little ups and downs, then it would have levelled out in a long straight line until just before he got out. Then it would have dipped right down again because he was scared of coming out. It's been very hard since he came out, there's no back up for a short sentence, being in there makes them paranoid, being paranoid ignites situations and makes them over react. He's been out for three weeks now and we've talked a lot, in a way we had to start from the beginning, I'm not being funny or dirty or anything but we used to talk about sex and thought we'd be at each other non stop when he got out, but we didn't do anything for days, it was psychological on Tommy's part, I was worried sick because I thought that I was failing him. He was so quiet and withdrawn, he would fall asleep at eight at night and wake at four in the morning and be wandering about the house, clattering around. He lost his job because of his conviction, he doesn't want another one now because he's used to doing nothing, he's not emotionally or physically ready for another job, it was a drink driving conviction and he's on one huge guilt trip. He finds it very, very hard to communicate now because there's no one to talk to in there. Things are getting there, but I was scared of him coming out, scared in case he'd changed and if he'd be a different person from when he went in."
Lucy 34, partner Tommy was sentenced to 5 months.

"My brother finally came home on tagging. It was really tough for us; my brother was one of the first to get tagged so we had TV cameras come into our home and film the whole thing. He didn't mind being tagged and he was actually totally different as a person although it didn't last. I don't think it helped him in any way. He developed this huge attitude problem, which made me even angrier.

"It felt very strange. The dog had died. The house totally changed."

> "You can't lose the focus of being a Dad. Listen to some of the younger kids in here and they are going to do everything as soon as they get out. But I've thought about it and I think it's best to spend time with the family and try making up for this time."
>
> *H. HMP Kirklevington 6 year sentence served 3, he has a son of 3 years old.*

I eventually started praying that he would go back to prison. After the tag came off he just went totally off the rails."
Kerrie 24, coping with her brother's release.

"I don't know what'll happen when he gets out, I don't like to think of anybody in jail so I go to visit him every week. When he gets out though, well, I don't know, things were not all that rosy before he went in, I would want it to work but I don't know. He might get a long time and anything can happen then can't it? yeah, I'll keep visiting him if he gets a long time."
Lena 25, has two children aged 7 years and 6 months, her partner is being held on remand.

"We are in a dreadful situation. He was on for tagging but because he hasn't got a permanent address he has to stay in for another four weeks at the end of his sentence. Probation are going to try and find somewhere for him to live. I couldn't take him back - I just wouldn't be able to cope with him. My daughter has actually offered to move out of our house so that he can move in.... but he stole from us, we even had to lock everything up around the house. We all feel very stressed. We've never had anything like this happen to us before." *Jill 47, talking about her teenage son who became an addict.*

On getting out:
Contributed by the writer in residence, and a group of writers, Kirklevington Grange.

"You feel as if you're being watched all the time. You feel vulnerable. You feel as if the word 'prisoner' is stamped across your forehead for everyone to see."

"I was always the breadwinner of the house, then I went home and the wife had redecorated the whole place - and I wasn't part of it."

"It's like starting again - like courting from the beginning."

"You go to this place called home, not where we used to live, a new area. You find yourself sitting in the front room, on the edge of the seat, tense as hell. You feel like a stranger. Treading into her space. Asking where the toilet is. The wife takes you round the house, shows you the rooms. They all look different. She seems wary. She thinks you might not love her any more."

"The kids were dead shy with me. Didn't want to know, went straight out to play. It's only me Dad."

"Couldn't have sex the second time."

"I couldn't even manage it the first."

"It's the day you've been working towards, and you have an image in your head, you build up things in your mind."

"I know one bloke booked a hotel room for the afternoon. Turned out to be a total waste of money."

"The friends all come crowding round, and all you want is a bit of peace and quiet at home. Everybody assumes you want to party. You can't turn 'em away because they're genuinely glad to see you."

"Don't expect to click in straightaway. Take your time to get to know each other."

"Just because I've been in the nick, some people think I'm a hard man. That reputation, it can be a burden to you. It's no use to me whatsoever. But still the young kids come round wanting to know, you know, what it's like in prison and all that rubbish. They've seen all this stuff on telly about Bronson and the Kray twins. They've almost been turned into heroes. The kids look up to you so you've got to put them straight. For God's sake don't admire me because I've been in prison. I've lost a hell of a lot more than I've gained. And that goes for Bronson and the Kray twins too."

"Don't expect the kids to obey you, there may be some resentment there. You have to earn their respect again."

"It felt very strange. The dog had died. The house totally changed. Mam has bought into a pub now. Of course I'm not allowed to go down there. It's never been my home."

"After being released from the 9 months and 4 years sentences I found it difficult at the beginning to 'connect' but the difficulty was mainly between my partner and I. My children were fairly young after my four-year sentence – the eldest being ten years. I found that if a problem arose the kids would go directly to their mother. If there was a negative response they would then come to me. I would go against the mother's wishes to keep them happy and I now realize that I was trying to gain 'brownie points' and approval from them. During the 2 years I was out, my partner and I came to a compromise, which was for me to stop over compensating for the time I was not around. I now realise that the real problems came after my 5 year sentence. With my two eldest a boy then 16, and leaving school and a girl of 13 reaching puberty. When I left my children were children,

"I had so much and I've lost everything. What I did was wrong in the eyes of the law, but I did it in temper and I'm paying the price now. My world has fallen apart but I'm not too old to change. I'm lucky I don't need to do much about my daughter. She's a good kid, her Mam does a good job with her."

M.25 HMP Loudham Grange sentence 8 years served four. Daughter aged 4.

"People sitting on the train look so ordinary. I feel like I stand out. It's like I've got 'con's wife' stamped on my head for everyone to see. But I don't feel that inside and I don't want our kids to feel crap about themselves."

very loving affectionate, always wanting to be near me, they hung on my very voice. When I returned 2½years later expecting to begin where I had left off, I was unhappily surprised to find no positive communication, no attention, very little love and most painful rejection! I found it hard to accept they were coping without me and were getting on with their individual lives. I felt like a complete stranger. I felt lonely and in despair in a place I regarded as my family home.

The biggest problem was with my eldest son who I believe resented me for trying to instill some type of discipline in him. My son and I began to have confrontations, which led to my partner and I having arguments, which led to my daughter and two youngest sons resenting me for upsetting the 'norm'. At this point I felt like a child. I felt as if I was walking on eggshells, trying to feel acceptance from family. My son and I hardly spoke for fear of saying the wrong thing leading to another confrontation or worse. I shed tears while writing that sentence: it was a very painful time for them and me.

I was asked to leave after another confrontation with my son. It left me in despair and I felt guilt for serving the prison sentences which I believe were the underlying cause of us drifting apart. I also felt anger at not being a competent father, resented, confused and lonely. Ultimately I used hard drugs and added another victim to my inadequate behaviour. I am currently awaiting another substantial sentence which has made a bad family situation much worse. I have also caused harm to an innocent member of the public which leaves me feeling insane. Hopefully my experience will help another mother or father cope with a similar situation in a more positive way." *Pete 35 years. Finishing off sentence and awaiting another.*

"For us, Michael coming home was easy, you tend to get used to doing everything, getting everything under control to do yourself, then you have to start letting go of things again when they come home. The first week was a honeymoon period, the week after, normal day to day. There was an incident in McDonalds when someone bumped into Michael and he almost jumped on him, it was a reaction, the way that he would have had to behave in prison, he would never have behaved like that before." *Jane 38, husband Michael was released on bail after being remanded in custody.*

"I had no worries about him coming home and we are fine, he came out on HDC and we had some problems with that, they have 'phoned us every night because we have a faulty box, they said that we must be moving it, I'm talking to my mother on the 'phone and they cut in to ask to speak to him to make sure that he's there. Some people are good though, like the man who came out to sort things out about the tagging, my little lad was being nosey and kept saying 'what are you doing?' the man said – 'I'm the Tele man." *Elaine 28, mother of three children aged 11, 4 and 2 years.*

"When he first came back I was more concerned about the tagging, that he wouldn't make his curfew cos of how he'd been up until going to prison but he accepted it and took the responsibility on himself. In those 8 weeks it was just me and him it was as though I was in control, he couldn't step out of line cos he'd go back in and we didn't argue once, it was brilliant. It was only when he came out of prison we started getting on, we're very close now. I'm starting to trust him more now, I worry when I see police cars that they are after him; I don't think you get total trust of them."
Lorraine 45, talking about her son.

Readjusting when released

" I think some women might resent the man being away and be frightened about them going back home. We do change. People could be strangers. Or some women could get used to their independence. They've had to make all the decisions and that can be hard on a man. That's where the course has helped me look at things from both sides." *S. 24, HMP Wolds.*

"My husband is now back. He used to play keyboard in a band but I told them that he had broken his back; I did that for him as I wanted him to be able to come back and carry on without being judged. Even now though we have to be careful what we say, have to keep lying." *Elise 35.*

"Since he has come home it has gone straight back to how it used to be which was great apart from the neighbour giving us loads of grief. *Claire 15, her Dad served prison sentence.*

"He came out on tagging, as he was one of the first, a film crew came along to film the process, but what I didn't like was they actually came into the house and went through every room in the house, toilet bedroom, and measured it all, which I wasn't prepared for. They were there for about an hour, an hour's induction then went all through the house with the film crew. I thought they would sit down with us and explain all about the curfew. He was quiet after they went; he didn't want to go out. During the 8 weeks, we were woken up all the way through the night by the tagging company phoning saying they couldn't find him, said it must be the duvet cover, we had his tag changed 3 times, the recorder box changed, they sat outside the house 'cos they couldn't get it right. I had more wires in my house than the electric company had! Totally unreal. But I

"There is so much to say but nothing to talk about."

"The whole thing was very embarrassing for me, the prison staff treat us visitors worse than they do the prisoners sometimes, we are not criminals!"

Lucy 34, visiting her partner Tommy.

found my son took it slowly and he adjusted to life and when the tagging was up he didn't go mad, it had calmed him down. If I had been prepared for the intrusion it would have been better but we didn't hear nothing apart from a phone call from Probation asking if I was prepared for him to come home early. We had no help from anyone apart from S.H.A.R.P."

Lorraine 45, her son was sentenced to two and a half years.

Released without support

"Anyway, he was given parole with only a couple of days warning because he had done his sentence and put back on the streets without any support or structure or guidance, I was distraught, I knew the system and I knew that he would get life this time. Tony had been released onto the street, no support plan, no back up, nothing and all the stuff he had just begun to address in Grendon, only scratched the surface of was left unresolved. (After some months Tony committed further offences and was given a life sentence.) I don't think its going to be hard with him on a lifer licence, he'll do fine and we'll do fine, he's never had anyone before, no one to come home to, nobody there for him but he's got me now."

Gina 31, supporting her partner through a life sentence.

Reflections

"I want a different life, but I'll miss out on everything with my daughter and my wife. I feel cheated of my life. There's nothing else I can say. I worry about my family all the time. Young Children can get poorly so easily. I'll never be there to cuddle her or help her. I wonder if 'phone calls will be enough, but at this age what can we do? I want her to have a good life. I had a happy childhood. Children should be with their parents. I wanted to be there when she was born. My family only tells me so much. I'm sure they don't want to upset me, but that only makes me feel worse." *J. 40, Loudham Grange, sentenced to 15 years served 2. Daughter is two and a half. Wife came over from India, she lives with his Mother who has cancer.*

"That's the thing about prison and punishment for your crime. It takes away the control you have, if any. It's a feeling of helplessness and not knowing. You really have to close your mind to things or you'd go insane. You don't realize the effect you have on your kids. It does make me feel hopeless and not responsible in the past. My wife saw to most things as I worked away from home a lot, but I provided all the money. I feel my life has been more hassle since we've had more money through me selling drugs. It's just not worth it all. I can say I wish things had turned out different, but we didn't complain at all the money coming in. But has it been worth it? It's so difficult to explain all the emotions and feelings you go through."
R.42, sentence 9 years served 3. Loudham Grange two daughters aged 14 and 16.

"When I contact them, (children) I take on their problems and I don't need that in here. I can't do anything to help them. Their photos are all over my cell but I don't like the scum in here looking at them."
Father of two teenage daughters. Loudham Grange.

"You hate the deeds he's done but you still love the child."

Speculation

written by a group of writers/performers at Swinfen Hall.

A man looked reflectively into the face of his son and saw himself staring back.

A man is the redeemed mistakes of a normal child.

A man hates being told what to do.

A man finds it hard to show his feelings.

A man loves his child.

A man should teach his child morals.

A man should be there for his child.

A man sees himself as a dominant person, but inside he is as vulnerable as the next person.

A man learns from his own mistakes and learns to take responsibility for his actions.

A man is not ashamed to admit he is wrong.

A man is not afraid to say sorry.

A man needs love.

A man can never be made.

A man is who you are.

A man knows little but learns much.

A man feels love but tries not to show it.

"I sometimes sit on the metro on my way to Durham just imagining I'm going to Durham to have a look around the shops - go to the Cathedral – like normal people. People sitting on the train look so ordinary. I feel like I stand out. It's like I've got 'con's wife' stamped on my head for everyone to see.
But I don't feel that inside and I don't want our kids to feel crap about themselves.

Their Dad feels crap enough for all of us. Who knows if this will be the last time inside? He hasn't got a job. It's become a way of life. That's awful isn't it?
I wish he could turn the clock back, but nobody can do that. I've questioned myself and him. I do get mad at him, just because I love him.
It doesn't mean I'm not mad at how our life is, maybe I should have left him, maybe I shouldn't have had so many kids, but I didn't leave and we had the kids.
We do love each other, but it's bloody hard." *JT. Visits husband in HMP Durham, she has 4 children, married 18 years.*

What Next

CHAPTER TEN - WHAT NEXT?

The voices in this book have described good practice and bad. They've shown the agony of the separation and the effect on their children. On the one hand some families have even been strengthened. But for most the effect has been catastrophic. If it is accepted that re-offending is reduced where strong family ties exist - it is vital to consider how to support families. But above all there is the human cost to children so vividly illustrated by these voices. The first step would be to acknowledge families - hidden and powerless - and to harness their strengths to rehabilitate their relative where possible. To do this, we need to consider who is affected:

Who is a prison parent?
347 people responded to our questionnaire in prisons. They told us that the following people were parents:
51% of young men aged 22 or under
90% of men 23 years and above
79% of women aged 22 or under
88% of women 23 and above

One in five prison mothers said
"I don't want my child to see me in here."
7% of prison mothers said their children did not want to visit.

Becoming a parent - a key moment to work with parents
It's definitely important for him to see the baby he is his Dad! The first he knew about the baby being born was when I took him on a visit the day after the birth, he was so shocked, but we had no way really of letting him know so we just took the baby in there. No matter how long his sentence will be I will still take my son in to see his Dad, I will always want him to know his Dad, he holds the baby the whole time on visits. The first time we took him in there, my other half was so shocked that he was born that he just sat there looking at him the whole time, couldn't believe it. He called me later to say sorry and everything for not giving me any attention and not asking was I OK and everything, it had all been such a shock to him."
Christina 25, visiting her partner who is remanded in custody, they have a three week old baby son.

What can prisons do for families? - support and inform
"What they need to do is make a package up for families of built up information, something that can help and guide you through everything because things change for everybody during the time somebody's in prison, I can understand why people split up, even more so if one of them has been away for a long time, it's because you're just left to get on with it."
Lucy 34, her partner received a first prison sentence, she has five children.

"Because the last time was so long ago I didn't know anything about the system – it had all changed, I didn't even know that you could get a reception visit until John's friend told me so I wouldn't have even got to see John so soon if it hadn't been for his friend, I would have sat at home and waited for a VO. At home only my friend and one of John's friends knew that he had gone inside, I didn't tell anybody. When you go to the prison you don't know anything, he had no baccy – nothing and I thought you could still take things in but you can't anymore, nobody told me anything." *Elaine 28, mother of three. Husband sentenced to 6 months.*

"I think the families should be informed a lot more, at any age, the parents should be informed at all times, I think the system is very cruel what the system does to parents, 'cos one minute they've got a son or daughter, the next they haven't, control's gone, and yeah there are a lot of parents that don't care but there's a hell of a lot of parents that do care. Even if the prisoner is messing about and in trouble, it would help them, come to terms with it." *Lorraine 45.*

"I had no problems 'phoning to book the visits but for anybody who has to travel the visiting times are useless, they are not organised to fit in with people's lives. If you have kids to take to school you can't make the 9.30 morning one – not unless you get there late and who wants to do that? You don't want to waste a minute of your visit and if you go for the afternoon one it's impossible to pick kids up from school." *Elaine 28, mother of 3.*

What we learned in the survey.

How happy are parents about their role?
86% of all the fathers questioned were happy to be fathers while fewer mothers felt the same –75% often because they felt the responsibility and the strain far more. Nearly one in four Mothers are likely to say they feel stressed about being a mother compared to less than one in ten of Fathers. (22.6% vs 8.2%)

How fathers feel
Fathers seem very confident that they are good with kids – nearly three quarters of them think they are. Are fathers overstating their competence? Few fathers felt the responsibility of a child was too much to deal with, but one in seven prison mothers felt that it was as they struggle to retain their role as the main carer for their child. A third of men were keen to hear about other people's experiences, while as many as half thought other people could benefit from hearing their own personal story. Fathers were fairly equally divided between those who felt they had learned about being a father from someone and those who had not.

"I think more focus should be given to parents and prisoners, the contact should be better. Visiting areas could improve, but it's good here. Parent's and children's relationships should be made a priority. The children come first."

S. 24 HMP Wolds.

The mother's role and the child's rights

When a mother goes into prison, emergency arrangements are more likely to be made for her children than when fathers are imprisoned. This could mean relatives or a care arrangement. In contrast to the increasing emphasis on children's rights, almost half of the children of prison mothers had no say in the arrangements made for their care. In interviews, women repeatedly said that they were 'bad mothers' and drug addiction was a common reason for this. They tended to blame themselves heavily and adopt a huge burden of guilt.

This showed in the survey too: The proportion of mothers who think they are 'good with kids' is far lower than the fathers. As few as 38% of mothers feel confident, while as we saw above, nearly three quarters of fathers said they were good with kids. 14% of mothers felt that the 'responsibility was too great.' More than half the women were nevertheless eager to hear or read about the experiences of other people who were away from their children and thought they might learn from this.

A very small number, 2.5% of people, thought that 'children today are out of control.' Instead, more than two thirds of prison parents believe that 'you should listen to kids and try to understand them.' Around 6% believe in smacking.

Contact

79% of fathers are in contact with the mother of their child compared with only 52% of mothers who are in contact with their child's father. Older fathers tend to be more likely to be in contact than younger Dads and among them, this figure rises to 83%. This makes it far more likely that men will get visits from their children via the mothers of their children than women do. Two thirds of prison fathers get to see their children. But for mothers in prison, fewer men visit with children or keep in touch. Less than half the mothers got visits from their kids. But one in five prison mothers said, 'I don't want my child to see me here' and 42% said "My child wants to visit me but cannot."

Mothers are more frequent letter writers to their children than fathers – 80% write and 73% 'phone their children. Only 58% of fathers write to their children and 54% 'phoned. Prison mothers still feel they have the responsibility for the family carrying on without them and more than three quarters of them were desperately worried about their family managing in their absence. Fathers worry too, but women are more likely to say they feel things are going wrong at home without them, while men tended to say they were confident that their Mum or girlfriend, wife or baby's mother was doing a good job. As so many men said this in the survey and interviews - in almost identical words - it seems this might be a way of letting themselves off the hook slightly. If she is doing such a good job, the argument goes, then my being here is not doing so much harm.

Release - unrealistic expectations

Questioned on what it might be like on release, two thirds of both men and women said it would be 'great'. But women were more than twice as worried about financial difficulties on release as men. A small number of each sex thought that a child might be jealous when someone returns home. Perhaps more adults should talk this through as children can often feel displaced. Questioned about useful help they'd received on subjects they'd need, our respondents appeared under informed especially the prison mothers. Preparation for release should include some realistic ideas about what must be worked out in the family relationships to help with re-integration.

Useful information.

Only 12% of women and 25% of men said they'd received useful information on practical childcare. It seems that men are more often given information on employment than women with a wide discrepancy showing up in their replies: 29% of men had been given useful information on employment compared to only 10% of women. 58% of either sex were eager to be given more effective advice on employment and 40% of either sex wanted to learn more about practical childcare. Over half the men and women had received no useful help on how to get on with children and partners.

But almost a quarter of prisoners felt they'd been given too much information on contraception. Women were extremely concerned about housing and 59% wanted more information on it. Women were also very keen to hear anecdotal advice on how other people coped in their situation.

More information beforehand?

"I wish I had had more contact with the barrister, as we didn't meet him until we got to court; we only had 5 minutes with him. If I'd known more about it I could have done a lot more for him, character references, to find out where he was, as at the time it was like bereavement. We didn't know anything at all. I think someone should prepare you for what's going to happen. We need to know what prison entails. You don't know whether he will be beat up, if has clean clothes, needs toiletries, he had no money on him, but I found out after what he could have taken with him." *Lorraine 45.*

Foreigners: should they be treated differently?

"Prison punishes your family – not just you – this cannot be right. I can't imagine by the time I get out of here what my oldest children will be like. Will I know them? I write to them often in Dutch. They are kids – they don't want to have a relationship where you can only write to your parents. I 'phone when I can, but there are no special circumstances for people from other countries and it costs so much. I think it is worse if you are not in your own country. You have even less control as a prisoner than normal." *J. 43, HMP Wolds.*

"You hate the deeds he's done but you love the child."

A 'wish list' for improving prisoner/family contact.

- To have visitors centres operational during times that suit families' needs.
- To review booked visits systems.
- To promote best use of visitors centres, i.e. use them as the valuable resource that they could be.
- Procedures for co-ordinated travel (for example) mini bus from town centres to prisons.
- Allow prisoners more freedom of movement within the visiting area for contact with children.
- To ensure that visitors are given their full entitlement to visiting times.
- Review 'who is eligible' for assisted visits in line with modern family life.
- To consider distances for family travel when deciding on a prisoners location.
- Provide more effective family services at visitors centres eg. Counsellors, advice workers.
- Provide dossier information to GP's etcetera on release.
- Have family visits for all young people (over 16 rule)
- Improve current systems for 'phoning home.
- Provide 'at the gate' support, ensure back up for those being released.
- Improve staff training for dealing with visitors.
- Improve standards in education departments.
- Discourage visitors centre staff from wearing prison badges and key chains.
- Improve system for accumulated visits and ensure they take place.
- Increase opportunities for children on visits to have a photo taken with parent.
- Better information to family immediately after sentencing.
- Better notification to families when prisoner is moved.

MOST IMPORTANTLY, INTRODUCE FAMILY/ PRISONER WELFARE OFFICERS AND UTILISE AND MAXIMISE THE POTENTIAL OF VISITORS' CENTRES. THEY COULD SERVE AS A BASE FOR VOLUNTARY GROUPS AND A RANGE OF AGENCIES PROVIDING SUPPORT AND HELP ON VARIED MATTERS.

In March 2002 the prison population topped 70,000, triggering wide awareness of overcrowding. The corrosive effect on rehabilitation was aired but few thought about the legions of children and family members affected by the imprisonment of a relative or close partner. 125,000 children are thought to be affected. Well over 11,000 prisoners were held more than 100 miles from home causing immense suffering to children and families. And 25,000 offenders are held 50 miles from home. Their children miss school and have their lives further disrupted as whole days are taken up by prison visiting. Financial hardship for the family is exacerbated. Few can keep a job and visit. Alternatively they may not visit at all due to the distance. Yet all the research shows that the closer prisoners are kept to their families, the greater the chance of reform.

Crime has been falling for the past 5 years, a 33% drop since 1996 to the lowest level since the British Crime Survey began in 1981. Despite this however, larger numbers of young people and children have been imprisoned and far more women. The effect on children when a mother is held in custody is stark. While we call for the provisions of the Children Act (1989) to apply to young people in prison, we should not overlook the children of prisoners. Their fate is often decided without their knowledge or consultation and they appear to have few if any rights.

The sentenced female prison population doubled between 1992 and 2000, while the pattern of female offences hardly changed according to research by Carol Hedderman of South Bank University, now working for the Home Office. One in seven of these imprisoned women are foreign nationals.

More than half of young prisoners on remand and almost one third of sentenced young offenders have a diagnosable mental disorder according to the Chief Inspector of prisons. Prison staff struggle to cope without adequate training where mental health professionals would be appropriate. But our survey found that half of young people in prison also have a child. Here and there, like beacons in the dark, some really good work is being done to prepare them for a future as a caring parent. Here and there too some prisons treat families well and the voices in this book are testimony to what a difference that can make. But of the system as a whole, we can only ask – are we brutalising or rehabilitating our citizens and their children?

Young Voice 2002

ADFAM - National charity for families of drug users
Waterbridge house, 32-36 Loman Street, London SE1 OEE Tel 0207 9288900

AFTERMATH - Nationwide support and counselling for families of those accused of serious offences. PO Box 414, Sheffield S4 7RT

BARS - support group for prisoner's wives
c/o Woodhill Visitors Centre, Tattenhoe Street, Milton Keynes, Bucks, MK4 4DA Tel 01908 501999

CHILDLINE - 0800 1111

CHILDREN'S LEGAL CENTRE - advice on children's rights 0207 3596251

DRINKLINE - 0800 917 8282 helpline

FEDERATION OF PRISONERS' FAMILIES SUPPORT GROUPS -
Unit 102 Riverbank House, Putney Bridge Approach, London SW6 3JD email: info@fpfsg.org.uk
Tel 0207 384 1987.

GET CONNECTED - 0808 8084994 Finding young people the help they need.
Free confidential helpline puts you in touch with the help you need.

IT'S NOT YOUR FAULT - website for children whose parents are parting. www.itsnotyourfault.com

HARPLINE - 0800 3893003 Help and Advice for Relatives of Prisoners managed by Ormiston Children and Families Trust.

HALOW - help and advice for lone offenders wives
PO Box 7081, Birmingham, B18 4AN Tel 0121 5519799

HEALTH HELPLINE - 0800 665544 provides information and advice on any aspect of health. Has national database of self-help groups.
Mon-Thur 9-7 pm, Fri 9-5 pm.

HEALTH WEBSITES - www.mindbodysoul.gov.uk and www.lifebytes.gov.uk

LIFELINE - freephone helpline for parents whose children are using drugs. Mon- Thur 4-8 pm 0800 716701

NACRO - National Association for the Care and Resettlement of Offenders.
169 Clapham Rd London SW9 010. Tel 0207 582 6500

NACCC - National Association of Child Contact Centres,
Minerva House, Spaniel Row, Nottingham, NG1 6EP Tel 01159484557 safe and supervised contact.

NACAB - National Association of Citizens' Advice Bureaux
115 Pentonville Road, London N1 9LZ Tel 0207 8332181

NATIONAL DRUGS HELPLINE - 0800 776600 free 24 hr free and confidential service, information, advice to callers with concerns about drugs and solvents.

The NEW BRIDGE - creating links between the offender and the community. 27A Medway St, London SW1P 2BD
Tel 0207 9760779 Family matters courses for prisoners, resettlement support and befriending. Branches: Dorset and Durham.
The New Bridge, P.O. Box 2364 Swanage, Dorset BH19 2YT and The New Bridge Volunteer Centre, Clarence Terrace,
Chester-le-Street Durham DH3 3DQ Tel 0191 3886069

OUTMATES - support for families, partners, friends of prisoners. 0208 6659562 24 hr helpline. Support friendship and understanding.
Physical support at court or just listening. Meetings one to one or groups. Telephone counselling. Lifeskills courses, Children's
activities.

PARENTLINE PLUS - 0808 8002222 Freephone helpline for parents.

POPS - Partners of prisoners and families support group,
St Marks Cheetham, Tetlow Lane, Cheetham, Manchester M8 7HF Tel 0161 740 8600

PRISON LINK - for families of Black and Asian prisoners (very active – drive families to prisons, services for children etc.) 29 Trinity road, Aston, Birmingham B6 6AJ Tel 0121 551 1207 emergency help line 0121 523 0695 (evenings)

THE PRISON REFORM TRUST - Research, Education, Information. Tel 0207 251 5070 (not a helpline)
15, Northburgh St, London EC1V OJR email prt@prisonreform.demon.co.uk www.prisonreformtrust.org.uk

PRISON WATCH - support/advice for prisoners and families, especially those at risk, assists also in cases of self harm, suicide, death in custody. 24 Rochester Close, Derby DE24 OHS Tel 01332 756158

PRISONERS' FAMILIES AND FRIENDS - Advice, drop in, holiday activities – free helpline 0808 8083444

PACT - Prison Advice and Care Trust – Family Support Services 254 Caledonian Road, Islington, London N1 ONG Tel. 0207 2783981 provides visitors centres at Holloway, Pentonville, Wormwood Scrubs and Belmarsh.

RELEASE - Drugs and legal advice 0207 7299904

SAMARITANS - 08457 90 90 90 Textphone 08457 909192 email jo@samaritans.org

SEXWISE - helpline 0800 282930

SCOTLAND - Prisoners' Families Information Line Freephone 0500839383 Answerphone 7 days 24 hrs We aim to respond to all calls within 2 working days. For advice about travel expenses, prisoner location, emergency help, visits, and specialised local services.

SHARP - Support, Help and Advice for Relatives and friends of Prisoners. Sharp, 83a Wyk Cop Shrewsbury, Shropshire, SY1 1UT Tel 01743245365 email sharphilary@hotmail.com
www.S-H-A-R-P.org.uk

SOFA - Advice for families of serious offenders
2 the Chestnut, Ellis Street, Hull HU5 3AR, Tel 01482 442133

TSA - Trust for The Study of Adolescence for a wide range of useful publications about teenagers.
Publications Dept. 23 New Rd. Brighton BN1 1WZ Tel 01273 693311 (not a helpline)

YOUNG MINDS - 0800 0182138 Free service for people worried about the emotional well-being of their child.

Young Voice works with young people to make their views and concerns heard. Research, projects, publications and representation. We are preparing a leaflet for families of prisoners. Among our publications are:

Bullying In Britain - Testimonies from Teenagers
Parent Problems! - Conversations with children when parents split up.
Good To Talk? - New ways of seeing children during and post divorce.
Thwarted Dreams - Young Views from Bradford.
Leading Lads - what do 1400 young men think of life in Britain today?
Can-do Girls - 3000 young women describe growing up in Britain.
The Gap - is a video pack with resource book and parents' booklet. For parents trying to help teenagers with their future.

To order tel 02089794991. www.young-voice.org

Published by Young Voice 2002

Registered Charity no 1078319

Copyright Young Voice

A catalogue record of this book is available from The British Library

ISBN 10903456-09-06

Concept by Adrienne Katz
Designed by Profile Design, Chichester .